ADHD Chronicles

47 Years of Extra Explained

These are my memories, from my perspective, and I have tried to represent events as faithfully as possible.

ISBN 9798862911275

Dedication

To my brother, my ride-or-die.
I wouldn't want to be the AD to anyone else's HD.
Love you, Chin!

Contents

ADHD - Attention Deficit Hyperactivity Disorder

Adult attention-deficit/hyperactivity disorder (ADHD) is a mental health disorder that includes a combination of persistent problems, such as difficulty paying attention, hyperactivity, and impulsive behavior.

Adult ADHD can lead to unstable relationships, poor work or school performance, low self-esteem, and other problems. Though it's called adult ADHD, symptoms start in early childhood and continue into adulthood. In some cases, ADHD is not recognized or diagnosed until the person is an adult. Adult ADHD symptoms may not be as clear as ADHD symptoms in children. In adults, hyperactivity may decrease but struggles with impulsiveness, restlessness, and difficulty paying attention may continue.

From *mayoclinic.org* (with some added Oxford commas...)

Preface

I don't expect this book to have readers past my brother and my husband. That's alright, though... I'm not writing it to make a profit or sell numerous copies of it. Writing has always been a safe haven for me, somewhere I can escape my imperfections and have everything *exactly* how I like it.

I've loved writing since I was young. I remember being itty bitty enough to ride around standing up in the front seat of my grandma's car – and making my own lyrics to songs that played on the radio. In high school and college, I often wrote lyrics to popular music and biographical poems when I needed a break.

When I got married, I made up children's stories that featured our sweet pup, Marlee. When I was battling infertility and later miscarriage, I wrote *"devotionals"* for myself as a means of healing. Writing has always been a way for me to express my emotions. When I was "hitting my stride" (or so I thought!) as a Realtor, I considered a *"You Won't Believe This Really Happened, But It Did!"* book. I started a book on lessons for new agents about important things they don't teach you in real estate school. I probably have half a manuscript of

"This Is How I Screwed Up, and I Hope You Can Learn from It" material. Who knows, maybe that will be my next project?

As much as these scribblings, notes, and ideas are a timeline of my life, I have always felt we go through things primarily to help others. Now that I am a mama to three wonderful children, I want to be my unedited, raw self and be proud of it. I always tell them, *"God created you this way because He wants you this way."* Hence, why can't I do what I have always loved to do (write) and practice what I preach?

This book is about me being *me.*

Just. Me.

It's not easy. I want to be real, yet I find myself changing aspects of myself. I often catch myself being a certain way and toning down parts of my personality as I feel like I come off too strongly at times to some people. Nonetheless, it's time I put my money where my mouth is. Who knows? Maybe by being intentional about being real, which is what I tell my kids to do, I just might find my peace.

I hope that putting all these thoughts and stories into a book will empower others to accept themselves as they are. I have always been a little *"extra,"* a lot, maybe - and now I know why. I feel like maybe it is time to embrace it and accept that this is, quite simply, Amanda.

For my 47th birthday, I received an unexpected present - a diagnosis of ADHD. Since my diagnosis, so many things have clicked that never did before. So much of my childhood and struggles throughout my life make sense now… traits that were commonly described as *"perfectionist," "sensitive," "emotional,"* or *"driven."* Even now, with a formal diagnosis, I speak to former teachers and colleagues, and they have trouble accepting that I was anything other than just "an overachiever."

As the mama of two boys and a girl, I have seen how society treats the same characteristics in boys and girls extremely differently. Between this and my personal research on ADHD *(and much therapy!),* I cannot help but wonder how many women remain undiagnosed and/or misdiagnosed - girls who never receive the support they need in order to reach their full potential. That is simply not acceptable.

I can hear you now. *"Amanda, you have SUCH a wonderful life… what are you talking about?"* From the outside and looking in, I may seem like I have it all together. I have an adoring and incredibly handsome husband who thinks I am the bomb, three bright, gorgeous kids who adore their mama (at least for now), a career that I love that evolves daily, and energy galore.

What I don't have, though, is what I might have been if I had been properly diagnosed as a child. Quite frankly, that infuriates me.

13

There, I said it.

As blessed as I am and thankful to God for what I do have, I know that I could have been and done so much more. *"No, please don't be so hard on yourself."* I can hear you now, the four of you reading this, anyway.

Clarity is power, and right now, I have clarity... clarity about so many things that have been a struggle for me that simply never had to be.

I will be fulfilled if this little book can help even one young girl receive the support she *needs,* one teenage girl realize that she is *NOT* too emotional, or one young woman accept herself as a beautiful creation of God in spite of what society or she sees as her flaws. As for the gray hairs (like me!), I hope you simply feel sisterhood.

Will some stories embarrass me or hurt my heart as I rehash them? Yes. However, I believe God wants us to help others through our own experiences. As a result, make a cup of coffee, sit back, and thank goodness you are not the person narrating these true stories. You may giggle, you may cry, you may roll your eyes and say, *"What in the world is she thinking?"* - but I promise you will feel something.

I feel like I'm rambling and getting nowhere. All I do is ramble! Welcome to my brain. This is what it is like with ADHD. Even when I try to calm down, my thoughts endlessly swim in circles. I hope that through my rambling, you can see a beautiful mess and accept some things about yourself that have always bothered you or others.

I am nowhere near getting to the level of acceptance I hope to achieve; nevertheless, I can be your cheerleader as you learn to accept yourself. Admittedly, I pray this book is a big step toward that acceptance in myself, as I want to model for my kids what it means to be true to how God created me. Just as I look at my kids and think, *"Oh, if they only saw what I see,"* I have to believe that the Lord does the same with me.

God made me this way. Period.

Time to embrace it.

Introduction

"Mama, the noise is driving me crazy."

I saw the text and looked up across the table to see my beautiful daughter, Elliott, trying to hold back her tears. We were sitting at the kitchen table discussing the fees for chorus, chrome books, and glue sticks. I wonder why they need these stupid glue sticks Every. Single. Year? My husband and son, Bradley and Parker, were talking about soccer, and Worth, my youngest, was being... well... Worth.

Lord, he's so extra! Anyway, she had already asked me twice whether I needed to go to the bedroom for some quiet time. I wasn't hiding that my nerves were so on edge that they were inside out. She and Parker are always in tune with how I feel, but I was determined to power through Day One of a new school year. It was the first night of how it will be throughout the year, for goodness' sake! The boys were exhausted from soccer, Bradley was fixing supper, and I was trying to help him catch up on sports director duties. As I helped Worth with homework (cause homework in kindergarten is SUPREMELY important to a five-year-old), I looked for the blessed checkbook to pay for a chorus shirt for Elliott. Chores had not been done, and I had to figure out the next day's schedule, showers, and so on, along with figuring out how our new routine would go. To top it off, dance hadn't even started yet! Lord, help us!

I stood there a while thinking, *"Amanda, if you can't get through tonight, we're all screwed."* Excuse the vocabulary, but that was my exact thought. Nevertheless, I did my little fidget finger trick to ground myself. I took deep breaths and stayed in the midst of it.

I could tell my little girl was on edge, though, so I told her to go take a shower. Showers are the absolute perfect excuse for glorious quiet! She looked at me with calm relief, took a deep breath, nodded OK, and quietly left the room. When she got out a few minutes later, I asked if she was OK, and she simply replied, *"Better."*

Well aware of her chores, she began putting towels away. Unfortunately, Worth was in the mood for the password game. My exhausted-wound-up-tight-as-a-tick tweenager had towels in her arms piled to the ceiling, and her little brother wouldn't let her through the door. She nicely said twice, *"Worth, let me through."* She didn't know the password, so how could he possibly allow that in his black and white "everything is a fun game" 5-year-old mind? Poor guy, he didn't realize a storm had been brewing.

She asked a third time, and that was my cue. I got up and raised my voice at Worth, only for *her* to burst into tears. Worth looked at her with utter devastation and confusion on his face. She quietly said through her tears, *"Worth, you just can't do that."*

My poor child. I could hear her voice shaking and cracking as she walked away. I walked into the bathroom to see towels everywhere, and my sweet little girl was standing against the wall with her head buried in one. She looked up and thought I was going to fuss. Nope. Not today, my love. Instead, I walked to her, patted her arm softly, and started picking up towels. She stood there sobbing.

A few minutes later, when the boys were upstairs, she entered the kitchen. I stopped her halfway to the sink and hugged her to remind her that I was proud of her. She got a glass of water and stood there shaking like a leaf. I said, *"It's a lot, huh?"* She nodded with tears threatening to spill over, took a deep breath, and started putting up the dishes.

This is ADHD.

It isn't always climbing walls, talking too fast, and zooming like you can't stop. Instead, it's being so overstimulated by things out of your control that every hair on your head – no, your *body* - is on end. Noises are magnified 100-fold, and a sickening tense feeling that you'll explode if you don't change environments *immediately* grows in your belly.

When she went to bed, she hugged me and said, *"I'm sorry, Mama."*

Oh, my beautiful butterfly, you have nothing for which to apologize. Mama gets it, and we will make it through this together.

Chapter 1: How It Began

I lost my keys in the great unknown.
And call me please 'cause I can't find my phone

This is the stuff that drives me crazy
This is the stuff that's getting to me lately.
In the middle of my little mess
I forget how big I'm blessed.

"This is the Stuff" Francesca Battistelli

I was first diagnosed at the ripe old age of 46. I, in my usual fashion, shared the news with the world. There isn't much in my life that is secret… and now I know oversharing is classic ADHD. And as I said, I truly believe that every challenge we face, in some way, shape, or form, can be used for good by God. So, I share. A lot. I immediately started getting A LOT of questions. I had folks asking how my diagnosis came about, what the signs were, etc. It is really hard to know where to even begin, so I will just jump in, and if I end up hopping all over the place, so be it.

When I was in high school, I was diagnosed with bipolar and OCD and put on medication. I was always super, super focused, and a perfectionist growing up. I wasn't happy with A minuses. I wanted an A plus. Nothing less.

I can remember the time back then when we used to call out grades to the teacher (thank goodness they don't do that anymore). This particular time I had a spelling test, and I got an 85 on it - I had NEVER gotten anything less than a hundred on a spelling test before! So, when I said "85" out loud, everybody in the room gasped because they were so shocked. I still remember one of the words was "chocolate" – – I had gone too fast and written "chocolata."

No, no, NO!

Anyway, I was so stressed and wound up about my grades all the time that this was a BIG DEAL. My sweet teacher even called me out in the hall and was like, *"Are you OK? Is something going on?"* Not only was it not typical for me not to make a hundred on my spelling test, but she knew I was having a breakdown inside. She talked to me for a few minutes and then told me to go to the restroom to take a break. Lo and behold, if I didn't throw up when I was in there!

I can look back and see so many instances over the years of times like this that I felt really deeply and things affected me in ways that they just did not affect other people. That's a silly little example, I know, but I think it's a good one. In girls, a lot of times, ADHD is not like the little boy who can't sit still and who's climbing the walls.

ADHD is hyper-focus. It may look like daydreaming, but it isn't. We are DEEPLY engrossed in our world and trying to make sense of it and be orderly, calm, and still. I am not a doctor, but in a nutshell– there are inattentive, attentive, and combined types. We haven't gotten so far with my diagnosis yet to determine what I am, but I'm leaning toward a combined type for reasons we can get into later.

Anyway, back to the timeline ... I was diagnosed with OCD and bipolar, and oh my goodness, looking back, I can see so many things that were red flags. There should have been indicators. Soooo many indicators. But we didn't know. Nobody knew. This wasn't talked about then, so I'm not casting blame on anybody or anything like that.

I remember things like tying my shoes ten times or so because I couldn't get the tightness of the two shoes equal. It was assumed to be OCD, but now I see it was sensory sensitivity. I remember leaning over and over and over and over again to make sure that my socks were lined up correctly because I was so paranoid about my appearance and how others perceived me. I felt anything less than perfection was failure. It wasn't that I needed the sock line to be straight for the sake of being straight - it was that I needed it to *feel* straight so as not to call more attention to myself. I remember erasing things in my notebooks to the point that there were holes in the paper because the handwriting wasn't neat enough. It wasn't that I wanted to be neat - I didn't want to disappoint the teacher. I had SUCH an intense need to please!

The irony is that now I am not like that at all. I am on the other end of the spectrum regarding neatness, accessorizing, and everything else. I often joke that my therapy and medication for OCD worked too well because now if I even get socks on both feet, I consider it a victory. (I don't even wear socks anymore, even with boots... but I digress!!). I'm NOT a neat freak. And goodness knows, you cannot read my handwriting. It's all over the place and changes from moment to moment. I can't even read it half the time! These are just a few examples, but so many things resonate with me now that did not resonate with child Amanda.

The common theme through it all is that it was *extra*. It wasn't hyper. It was hyper FOCUS. It wasn't being driven. It was extreme consciousness of things that didn't get to or didn't bother or affect other people. It was upset stomachs and headaches and shaking hands over seemingly silly stuff.

So anyhow, here I go. I'm squirreling. I'm supposed to be talking about my diagnosis and going into my life's history. But hey, that's what ADHD is, right? Squirrels everywhere. My friend Angele likens it to a million thoughts all flying around crazy like dollar bills in one of those air machines, but you can't catch any of them - let alone organize them. She wrote, *"It fits... you try to grab what you can, and most of the time, it isn't what you should have grabbed... you just need someone to turn the air off and give you time to pick them up and put them in 1s, 5s, 10s, 20s, etc. - hoping to get those 100s organized. The air machine is my life."* Truer words were never spoken! Anyhow...

For years and years and always, I was a top student, a top athlete, my high school's Student Body President, went to a great college (Go Heels), made good grades, and was president of my co-ed fraternity... alllllllll the things. I attended a year of law school, met my husband (my mama won't be happy if I don't point out here that our mamas got us together...), came home, got married, and the happily ever after began.

There are so many times I can remember looking at Bradley, or looking at my mama, or looking at my business partner, and being like, *"Why is my brain like this? Like, why don't I get this as other people do? Why is this so hard for me?"* or, the flipside - *"Why is this something that comes so easily to me? Seriously, why are other people struggling with this?"* Everything has always been extreme in all ways, from finances to organization to business to conversations to appearance - one end of the spectrum or the other - it is either tidy perfection or a disaster.

OK, moving along... we dealt with infertility for many years and ended up having three precious, precious, precious children. I also have two in heaven whom I cannot wait to meet one day. I have an adoring husband, and to the outside world, I am very successful in my profession. As far as everything and everyone is concerned, I'm happy, I'm fulfilled, and things don't get any better.

Hello, November 2021.

Backstory - my PA, whom I absolutely love and adore, had been telling me for a couple of years - probably since my youngest was about three years old - that she wanted me to go to therapy. I do not miss the timing on this. My youngest is a handful. He's a good handful - he is joy, love, and affection, but he gives us a run for our money in ways our two oldest did not. He's kind of extra. OK, he's a LOT extra. I see myself in him on the daily. Bless.

Anyway, I always chalked my fatigue and worry up to, *"Oh my word, I'm in my mid-forties, and I have a three-year-old who's a lot, and I have two older kids who are extremely conscientious about life in general, and I'm, you know, I'm trying to balance that with work. And I'm giving my husband time, my church time, my mama time, and my grandma time (I was her caretaker for three years), and I was just like, this is what we do."*

In my mind, I'm a 46-year-old woman with these things on my plate. But all 46-year-old women with three kids on their plates struggle with this stuff, so what's the big deal? I just didn't have time. I told her I would schedule an appointment, but it simply never got on the books. It wasn't defiance or ill intention but because it kept getting pushed to the back burner. Too many more important things to do!

Ummmm.

One night in November, I was at home with my youngest doing the dishes. He was in the living room playing - just happy as a lark! I remember thinking, *"Ah, what a nice quiet moment for once."* I started to feel this tightness in my chest, across my back, down my arm, and even down into my belly, unlike anything I had ever felt. I couldn't breathe. I literally could not take a deep, or even semi-deep, breath. It built really slowly, starting as burning and turning into this intense pressure.

On one shoulder, I had a voice saying, *"You're fine. Just chill out. Everything's gonna be OK. Just sit down and relax."* Then on the other shoulder, I had this voice saying, *"Oh my gosh, if something happens to you, your five-year-old will be by himself... in the house... at night. You know what? We gotta do something."*

So, I got on the floor, and I was on all fours and then doubled over. It was pain, but it wasn't like a stabbing pain or anything like that. It was a tightness, like I had something squeezing me. I called my mama and said, *"I can't breathe. I think I have had a heart attack. I need you to come to the house."* (Because, of course, as a mama, I had to insure my child would be cared for before calling 911!).

She, of course, immediately hit the road. I called 911, and by that time, I couldn't even get the words out. I couldn't even tell them I couldn't breathe or that I was having a heart attack. It was the scariest moment of my life. Thankfully they knew what was up and told me they were sending someone asap. I remember putting the phone down, and then Mama showed up in like two minutes (even though she lived seven minutes away!). When she got there, I was on the floor behind the couch (again, mama brain... I went behind the couch so my son wouldn't see me struggling), and when she walked in the door, I immediately lifted my hand. I didn't want her to see me on the floor and think I was dead because I couldn't get any words out. I couldn't get out, *"Mama, I'm OK, I've called 911"* ... anything! I just kept pointing to Worth. She figured out that I wanted her to take care of Worth. Just occupy Worth. I didn't want him to see me and get scared.

So anyway, 911 came, and they did all the initial testing. They did not see signs of a heart attack, but they could tell by my blood pressure and other vitals that I had something going on. They loaded me in the ambulance to go to the hospital. It really is like on TV when everything is hazy but bright. And they *mayyyyyy* have blown a tire on our dirt road... but I digress...

So, I get to the hospital, I get admitted, and I end up staying 3-4 days. I don't remember how long exactly, but it was several days. They were amazing... they gave me every test in the book - echo, EKG, stress tests, CT scan, MRI, everything. Nothing funky showed up, and I was released.

When I went home, I didn't know why it happened, but I knew it had happened, and they told me to follow up with my doctor. It absolutely scared me to death, so I did what I was supposed to do and made an appointment. I went in 2-3 days later, and Jennifer looked at me and said I was absolutely going to therapy. She felt I had a big overblown panic attack or anxiety attack or whatever and that I was going to therapy or she would stop refilling my meds. Gulp. She meant business. Even then, though, I was thinking, *"Panic attack? Panic over what? Anxiety over what? I have a lot on my plate, but I couldn't live a better life."* I wanted to be a good patient, so I made the therapy appointment.

It was about a week later and was a Zoom visit with a therapist in Lewisville. We discussed my medical history and talked through my present and past diagnoses and things like that. At the end of our VERY FIRST visit - literally after spending an hour with me virtually -

she asked if I had ever considered or been talked to about ADHD. I initially thought, *"But I'm not bouncing off the walls. I mean, I'm hyper and have a lot of energy, but I'm not that. I'm not like THAT. I'm not like those little boys who didn't get good grades because they couldn't sit still."* So, this was how the conversation started.

Our next few sessions were more exploration, and of course, I went to Dr. Google when all this was going on because that's what we do. We were digging deep into all these things in my past that had led to misdiagnosis and treatment of other things - things that were not the root cause but were possibly indicators of a bigger picture. She felt my ADHD tendencies had always caused me to be so extra, be it extra giddy, extra depressed, extra extra. Whatever had caused me to be a perfectionist and get up in the middle of the night to straighten pictures on the wall had then caused me to go the complete other direction to the extreme once I started dealing with some of those issues. Cause that's what we do. It's all or nothing. Insert facepalm emoji.

As I said, I don't put fault on anybody for the bipolar or OCD diagnosis. I think they definitely are there, but I'm not convinced that they did not start with ADHD and then were exacerbated by so many of the ADHD traits - eagerness to please, sensory issues, etc. I am not sure which is the chicken, which is the egg, or which is the chicken...

I am not insured, which ended up being a blessing because it meant I could go to whomever I wanted to go whenever I wanted to go. I don't have to get insurance approval. I don't need a referral blah blah blah. The problem was, though, that my therapist could not prescribe medication, so she sent me to a psychiatrist. I had the first appointment, and it was a mess. It was really hard to pin her down, for starters, and then the psychiatrist was late... things I found incredibly ironic for a therapist dealing with folks with ADHD. But anyway, that's another conversation. She was absolutely determined that I would stick with the original diagnoses and even made some comments like "ADHD in women is not common" and was very dismissive. Gee, thanks. I am still with my original therapist, though.

The biggest benefit to the diagnosis so far has been self-awareness. This has also been the biggest curse. I can look back, and I can say, for example, *"Oh my word, this is why I never could get ahold of our finances!"* While that's validating, it also makes me sad because it means it's final. At night, when I go to bed, I can't just think, *"OK, I'll get my act together tomorrow,"* because I'm not wired to get my act together. That is REALLY frustrating. There's a lot of work that has to be done and a lot of time and reprogramming that have to go into it. It explains why at work, I supposedly have my act completely together...I'm a top-producing agent, run a wonderful team, have repeat clients who remain loyal, am a real estate instructor, and people come to me with questions seeking advice and wisdom. I am respected in our office and my profession, but then at home, I'm exhausted.

It's like I have a bucket of energy; all my energy goes into work, being productive, focused, organized, and not dropping the ball for my clients and taking extreme care of them. Then I get home, and life is a fiasco. I joke that my kids have a great life because it's a zoo. My house is a disaster. My car is a wreck. All the kitchen cabinets are open, our finances are a mess... so many things. The pieces of the puzzle have come together, and it finally makes sense now. My husband hates the bucket analogy, but even he gets it - when my bucket is empty, it's empty. Period.

I've continued consulting Dr. Google, and as I read more and more about this, I'm finding this is very common among women. A lot of women in their late thirties and forties are being diagnosed who have probably had it all along, and there's a tragic lack of awareness around it.

So that's where I am.

I want to share. I don't want my daughter, either of my sons, or anybody I love to go through life overachieving yet feeling like they've never achieved enough. That's basically me in a nutshell. In school and athletics... in my professional life... I've always, always, always been an overachiever, yet I've never, ever been satisfied. I've never felt like it was enough. I've always felt like I could be better and like I was letting people down. I can't tell you the number of times over the years that Bradley has looked at me and asked how I don't see all that I've accomplished, and I'm like, *"No, honey, I don't."* Bless that man, but that's how it is. That is 110% indicative of our mindset and the way our brains work. *We are never enough. How sad.*

Chapter 2: Pivotal Moments

She is running
A hundred miles an hour in the wrong direction
She is trying
But the canyon's ever-widening.
In the depths of her cold heart
So she sets out on another misadventure just to find
She's another two years older.
And she's three more steps behind.

"Does Anybody Hear Her" Casting Crowns

When I began this book, it was basically to protect my Facebook followers from reading my middle-of-the-night stream-of-consciousness novels. I tend to go long, and by the time I add my ellipses, italics, bolds, and parenthesis... you get the picture. I write as I talk, so this may be better on Audible. Anyhoo...

I've thought a lot about different things that happened when I was growing up, and there are so many memories that finally make sense. For various reasons, things have stuck with me through the years, and now it's like putting together the pieces of a puzzle. An old Southern Gospel song talks about how we see the threads, but God sees the tapestry. As I look back on these things, I can see how God has woven together these individual threads to create a complicated, outside-the-lines, all kinds of colors (that shouldn't really go together but do anyway) tapestry.

That's my life since my diagnosis, and I'm having a lot of *'aha'* moments. It's enlightening when something hits me, and I realize, *"Oh, oh, NOW that makes sense!!"* There are so many examples, but for the sake of your eyesight, I will only discuss a couple.

I've talked about how, in girls, the traits indicative of ADHD are often very different from the traits in boys. Boys often can't sit still. They climb the walls and blurt out in class – they do things that get them in trouble. Young girls, on the other hand, commonly show more as extremely studious, very conscientious, and anxious... a lot of descriptions like she's *"motivated,"* she's *"driven,"* she's *"disciplined."* These terms are actually used as ways to praise us and encourage us. So, it becomes a never-ending cycle for us girls because the things that should indicate a deeper issue are praised and encouraged.

I want to go ahead and say right here that I'm not throwing stones at anybody. My husband thinks I walk on water, and he has always made me feel like the most loved wife in the world. My parents were coming from the right place when I was growing up and were doing it from a spot of *"We're proud of you, and we want you to be the best you can be."* My parents think I'm the bee's knees now and pretty much always have. I am confident in that. So, I hope and pray that as people are reading this, they realize that I'm not blaming anyone for anything in a negative way.

Whereas the things that they may have said or may have done, especially my mama, probably perpetuated and strengthened my ADHD tendencies, I don't blame them for that at all. Please just walk away from this knowing I am not angry. Well, not at people. I may have a little bit *(OK, a lot)* of anger toward the circumstances in general, but I'm not angry towards the people in my world.

Anyway, there was an incident when I was in kindergarten. I have thought about this many times over the years and returned to this very moment. I'm convinced it's one of the reasons that I've always been so conscientious about keeping my appointments and checking my calendar. It was toward the end of the school year, and I remember that because it was a day we got to change into shorts at lunchtime. We would wear our long pants to school, and then if it got warm enough, we got to change into shorts. I remember going into the little bathroom there in kindergarten and changing my shorts.

When I came out, the teacher told me I had not turned in a permission slip. I was like, *"Oh gosh, what permission slip??"* She reminded me that we had been given permission slips to get signed for a field trip that very day. I responded that it was in my cubby (and even as I am typing this, I feel sick in my stomach). She asked me to get it for her, and I remember walking back to my cubby with this intense feeling of dread. Number one, I didn't know if my permission slip was in my cubby, and number two, I knew that even if it was there, I hadn't taken it home to get it signed.

You know how in the movies time stops? I remember walking across the classroom, and of course, I felt like everybody was looking at me because that's what we do - we think we have targets on our backs. I vividly remember walking over to my cubby and pulling it out and rifling through things, and in the very, very back, creased and bent and balled up, was my permission slip - my UNSIGNED permission slip.

Remember that even in kindergarten, I was a model student. I did EXACTLY what I was supposed to do. I was pretty much the teacher's pet because I was so well-behaved, compliant, and eager to please. So, when I saw that permission slip, my stomach dropped, and my feeling went from dread to *"Oh my gosh, I'm gonna get in so much trouble."* The room started swimming, and I felt the tears start to well.

And you all remember - I was SIX. I was a six-year-old girl already feeling these intense, debilitating at times, emotional responses. I got my permission slip out and walked back across the room to the teacher. I handed it to her, and I remember so well that my little hand was shaking as I held it out. My teacher was sitting at her little table, in those teeny short-legged chairs that kindergarten teachers sit in (I don't see how in the world they sit in those things all day!). She unfolded it, and she was so disappointed. She looked at me and said, *"Amanda, this is not like you."* I immediately started crying crocodile tears and apologizing.

Thankfully, because I was such a good student, they just called my mama and told her what had happened. And again, they asked if I could go because I was such a good kid. I got to go on the field trip that afternoon, but what the teacher said always stuck with me (again, I am NOT knocking my teacher!). She told me she just wanted me to be the best I could be and that they expected better of me. I spent the entire field trip sick on my stomach and on the verge of tears. The. Entire. Trip.

I was miserable. I had let my teachers down. My teachers could tell I was upset before I got on the bus because they hugged me and told me they loved me. Even with that, I was torn up to the point that I couldn't sleep that night. I couldn't sleep because I had disappointed people that were important to me.

I was six. Six years old.

The next day was a Friday. On Fridays, we often did these fun awards like senior superlatives. They would give out certificates for an act of kindness, a good grade, the best coloring sheet, or always being on time for lunch or whatever. I don't remember what all the things were, but that morning I remember riding in the car and then the bus to school. I had on my knee-high platform boots, and they were covered in mud. We didn't live in our district, so our parents would drive us to the bus stop, and then my brother and I would ride the bus to school. The ride that morning was in slow motion.

Anyway, I remember sitting there in the car and then on the bus, and I didn't want to go to school. That never happened – I LOVED school. I dreaded seeing my teachers, and I just knew my classmates had spent all night talking about my screwup (remember the target on our backs?). When I got to my classroom, I immediately ran up to my teachers and burst into tears, apologizing again for disappointing them and promising it wouldn't happen again. I still feel to this day how they loved on me and hugged and reassured me. Mrs. Johnson even kissed my forehead. I fondly remember that they showed intense, intense love and compassion.

When they said it was certificate time that day after lunch, we all gathered and sat crisscross apple sauce. And I got a certificate! I was so excited! I hadn't gotten one in a while but got one that day for being "sweet as pie." I remember thinking, *"Well, that's funny, you know, you don't usually get it worded like that."* I was thrilled...until the worry set in.

After they gave them out, I went up to my teachers and told them I needed to understand. I ALWAYS needed approval and validation in everything I did, so I asked them why I had gotten it. I knew Mama and Daddy would ask, and they'd want to know if it was something specific. My sweet teachers responded that while they were upset that I didn't bring the permission slip back, they were touched and impressed by how much it bothered me. It showed that I was a really good person and a really conscientious student, and they were super proud of me - TOTAL reinforcement of the over-achieving, compassionate, extremely emotional, taking things harder than they should be taken character traits of a little 6-year-old girl who was really suffering from ADHD.

I resolved that day that I would NEVER forget another permission slip. I remember it like it was yesterday. I was standing at my class window, looking up at the big brick building that was the main hub of Forbush Elementary School. All the classrooms were in one big building except kindergarten and 1st grade. Kindergarten and 1st grade were in a little building out to the side. I remember standing there at the window and thinking to myself, *"I will never again forget another permission slip ever as long as I live."*

It wasn't due to pride, though.

It wasn't because I was proud of myself for getting the sweet-as-pie certificate. They felt like they needed to give me a certificate to make ME feel better. Ugh. In my six-year-old mind, I had hurt THEM! There was this constant perpetuation of guilt and anxiety and working crazy hard to achieve the right result, even though the result manifested an incorrect or inappropriate emotion. I am tired just thinking about it!

OK, so fast forward. I've talked about how things in girls cause us to be praised and oftentimes are reinforced and validated through that praise. Fast forward to my senior year of high school, and I received a progress report with three absences marked in English class. Mrs. Barlow was my teacher - her husband, Mr. Barlow, had been my history teacher the prior year and was my favorite teacher ever. He was really tough with super high standards, and Mrs. Barlow was more of the same. She was strict on her own, and because she was Mr. Barlow's wife, I really, really wanted to live up to her expectations. I was student body president, I was the volleyball player, I was this, that, and the other, and I was a teacher's kid... I was everything, and I felt like I had more than a lot expected of me. I had big shoes to fill, even though those shoes were created in my own mind.

And so, it's toward the end of the school year - I think it was probably 3rd quarter? I got my progress report, and it said I had three absences. Well, I had NOT had three absences. I knew I had not and was going to fight for my attendance record! So, I went to Mrs. Barlow immediately and told her I had not had three absences. I was probably sassy in my righteous indignation, but she was very gracious and said, *"Well, if you can show me the dates and figure out where you were, then we'll mark those off."* Bless Mrs. Barlow.

I immediately returned to my desk and pulled out my little calendar (one of those purse calendars we used back before technology). I walked back up to her desk, and she gave me the dates of the marked absences. My calendar was kept not just as a calendar but also as a diary, so it was FULL of details. I was able to look at the dates for every single one and tell her EXACTLY where I had been and what I had been doing - even to the minute. I even knew that on two of the days, we had substitute teachers and who they were.

As student body president, I got out of class all the time. It was fabulous. It drove my teachers, especially my Latin teacher Mr. Rowland, absolutely nuts. I got called out constantly (did I mention that it was fabulous?). But I was able to tell her to the minute what I had been doing. One day I was showering after an assembly where we showcased our volleyball skills by playing this one-man team who only won because he carried the ball like it was a baby...but I digress. Another day my tardiness was due to showing a new special needs student around campus. I don't remember the 3rd one, but by the time we got to it, she said, *"You know what, anybody that's as organized and conscientious as you are, I'm going to take their word for it that if they say they were at school, they were at school."* I got credit for all three days. BOOM!

So again, my extreme habit of chronicling everything I did and obsessively writing down every detail was reinforced and turned into a positive. When I say that I had those things on my calendar, I didn't just have those things on my calendar. I would go back to my calendar at night and write in things that had happened during the day, not to help me keep appointments but as a diary so that if I ever needed details, I had them. So so so eager to please and paranoid all the time! On those little twelve-month calendars, the daily squares were only inch by inch; I would actually make extra pages that I would then staple or tape into my calendar that could be a continuation of certain days. Not only did I have to write down everything to make it happen, but if I missed something, I had to go back and write it down after the fact.

Remember how I said I would never forget another permission slip? My little purse calendar saved me in that particular circumstance. It sounds silly, but this is indicative of how I took that little promise I made to myself as a six-year-old and went to the other extreme with it.

43

Our society sees that as positive, and it IS a positive. I'm not trying to knock society or anything like that, but it's a perfect illustration of how the things that are problematic for girls and are indicative of potential ADHD, anxiety, depression, obsessive-compulsive disorder, etc...... those things in us are PRAISED and encouraged to flourish!

Even to this day - to this very day! - if I have to fill out a permission slip for my kids, turn paperwork in for them, turn paperwork in for taxes, or anything like that, I'm taken back to Ms. Bryant's kindergarten classroom or my senior year in Mrs. Barlow's class. I can feel myself handing over that permission slip with shaking hands or my adrenaline pumping as I walked back to my desk to get that calendar. There was no way - there was NO WAY! - I had three absences, and I had to prove it because I had to have perfect attendance.

A lot of times when I give my kids their permission slips or order forms or whatever, I'll say seven, eight, nine times, *"Make sure you turn this in!"* I will even email the teacher to tell them I gave it to my child. Then, when they get home, I'll ask if they turned it in (*"Are you SURE you turned it in??"*). I know I drive them crazy (because I drive myself crazy), but that's baggage, I guess, from my childhood and ADHD. Thankfully, they roll with it.

These examples may seem silly. If you're reading this and it seems silly, be thankful. But if it doesn't seem silly and resonates at all, you get it. You know that feeling of literal nausea because you disappointed someone...that self-talk of *I'm a horrible person, a terrible student, a bad girl.* Those things were never said to me at all. They were never ever said to me from an external source, but those were the words that constantly rang in my head. So, I was always, always, always trying to achieve the next pinnacle of perfection.

Thankfully, on the surface, it all turned into good. It grew into being extremely conscientious and not dropping the ball in my work. I may pay a bill late, but I don't miss dates for my clients. I don't mess up my paperwork or have paperwork issues. My paperwork is beautiful. It's filled out and thorough — it's just GORG. I am always ahead of the transaction as far as my dates go when I have properties listed and in escrow. My executive function <u>at work</u> is HIGH, but I guarantee you that I feel and experience more negative thoughts and physical manifestations than most. No matter how well I do, I have a constant sense of *"I can do better. I can be better. I'm not doing my best, etc."*

I will go to bed at night and pray, *"God, please help me be better tomorrow."* Thankfully I think the Lord honors that we want to be better people as far as our character, morals, and that kind of thing go. But I have to wonder sometimes if the Lord isn't looking at me like I look at my kids and thinking, *"Honey, you're perfect just the way you are. Please, please, please stop worrying."* I know that's what I think of

MY kids, and I just can't help but think that the Lord is probably looking at me that same way. It goes back to the tapestry, and I don't mean to get all preachy here about it, but I feel like the Lord wants me to use this for good.

He has put this diagnosis in my life and these realizations of all these puzzle pieces fitting together for this time and for this purpose.

Such purpose.

My ramblings can potentially help another little girl be understood or help someone's parents or teachers understand them a little better... understand why that little girl is so anxious, worried, cries so easily, and is so eager to please. I don't want anybody, any little girl or boy, to ever have to walk to their cubby with the feeling of dread that I had. That's just not a place that any six-year-old should be.

It just all makes sense now. There are so many other examples that I can look back on that fit the pattern. I wonder, are there things in your life... in our lives that we can look back to and see time stand still. How did those things mold us? How did they make us the people that we are today? Especially little girls.

Suppose you have that little girl who is extremely conscientious, extremely driven, and extremely motivated. In that case, I encourage you to examine that and look at her from the perspective of, *OK, are these things caused by anxiety? Are these things caused by an almost irrational sense of needing to be perfect?*

Because if they are, your little girl is suffering, and that's no fun.

Chapter 3: Superpowers

'Cause I got a couple of dents in my fender
Got a couple of rips in my jeans
Try to fit the pieces together.
But perfection is my enemy.
And on my own, I'm so clumsy.
But on your shoulders, I can see
I'm free to be me.

"Free to be Me" Francesca Battistelli

I frequently have people reach out from my Facebook posts and tell me how my anecdotes have helped them better understand a grandchild or a coworker. So many of them see the negative or problematic side of ADHD... however, there ARE positives. In a lot of ways, ADHD *is* my greatest gift. Do I forget that sometimes? *Absolutely.*

SOO much of what makes me "me" is directly related to my diagnosis. I still get angry that I was not properly diagnosed and get mad when the ADHD is raging... alright, let's focus on the "hashtag bright side!"

So, this chapter will be about the superpowers of ADHD and what it allows and empowers me to do, which I truly do not believe I could do otherwise. Granted, many of these can work in reverse, but today is about the positive. I hesitate to call them *"superpowers"* - this is yet another example of our society feeling the need to sugarcoat EVERYTHING. Instead of *superpowers*, I like to call them *gifts*. I recently saw a documentary where a lady said that she felt that her ADHD was one of her greatest *gifts*.

BINGO! I love that perspective!

A gift isn't always a blessing, while a superpower is. I know my mama has the gift of listening, which on the surface is *wonderful*... until the 17th stranger of the day opens up to her about their addiction, financial struggles, etc., and she gets so burdened with other peoples' issues that it brings HER down. That's how I look at my ADHD; hence, calling these "gifts" is the spin I will use. Society likes to paint fluffy unicorns on everything, though, so the chapter's name is one to which most will relate.

I have several talents that, were it not for my ADHD, I don't think would be used for good. For starters, and this is not about any specific thing - it's a combo of 1100 things — I definitely don't think I would have been as good a real estate agent for all these years as I've been if it were not for my ADHD.

If you are in real estate, you know that this career and this industry require us to wear many hats, and sometimes we have to wear *ten* hats in a day and change hats on a moment's notice with zero warning. My ADHD has helped me take some of those things, some of that instability, lack of consistency, and spontaneity (so to speak!), and turn them into positives.

These positives have fueled a great career, and I'm really thankful for that. Since I have been so open about my diagnosis, I have found out there are several folks in my world in the same boat. And honestly, most of them are rock stars - well, rock stars on the surface, anyway. Many of them struggle with the same things I do - extreme empathy, financial disorganization, etc. But then again, this is a bright-side chapter, so I will hush!!

So on to the formal *"list"* - you know we ADHD'ers love lists!! OK, here goes...

Number one - I am creative.

I'm not creative in like a Pinterest way, i.e., I'm not creative in that my kids' birthday parties should be posted in magazines and things like that. My idea of a birthday party is to order a sheet cake from Lowes, go to the dollar store and get some Paw Patrol figurines, and then put those figurines on top of the cake. That's about as creative as I get with the cakes. Decorations are balloons and napkins from Party City, so there is nothing to send to Martha Stewart. However, I am creative in thinking of ways to handle situations that would otherwise be problematic.

Recently, I was at a dance competition with my daughter and got her some rice from Bojangles. She LOVES some Bojangles rice, just like her mama! They didn't give us a fork, and she was panicking about it. I was like, *"Babe, don't worry about it... just take the lid off the water bottle and use it as a scoop. There you go. Voila - you have a spoon!"* So simple to me, yet the other dancers and their moms were flabbergasted at the genius of it.

When both of my bigs were creating volcano projects for school, they got REALLY upset that we ran out of red paint. Mama to the rescue! *"Who cares? We have nail polish, ketchup, and hair spray! There's your lava!"* OK, that may not sound like a big deal, but I can very quickly come up with alternative ways to get things done. No panty liners? *Grab a baby washcloth.* No eyeshadow? *Just dab a tish of lipstick on your finger.* No celery for the casserole? *Throw in some water chestnuts.* There is ALWAYS a way to make things work!

Often, I come up with silly little slogans and jingles in our marketing and community outreach. This is ridiculously goofy, but *I* thought it was cute... at the end of the school year, we gave the teachers at several schools prizes every week in recognition of teacher appreciation month. We had these silly little jingles that went with our displays. One of the weeks, we gave all the teachers these little packets of fruit chews. It was the last week of the school year, so the little *"jingle"* on the sticker was *"Tooty Fruity, it's Time to Scooty!"* I know that's goofy, but goofy things like that make people smile... I'm pretty good at that stuff, and I think that's pretty cool. Just remember, though, if you're going to ask me to do place settings for a birthday party or baby shower, you're out of luck there.

Number 2 - I have crazy strong intuition.

I'm not going to go into specifics because I don't want to tell on myself (or others!), but there have been so many times since Bradley and I have been married that I have met somebody at a work function, a ball game, or a family gathering. When they've walked away, I've looked at him and given him a quick opinion on the situation, and he's been like, *"No, what are you thinking? Where did that come from?"* And then, lo and behold, six months down the road, he calls me up, and he's like, *"Oh my word, you TOTALLY called it."*

I hear that A LOT. I've read that intuition is very strong among those of us with ADHD. We're really in tune with listening to that little voice on our shoulder and the hair on our neck standing up and that kind of thing.

Number 3 - I am really good in a crisis.

Well, except for the time that my son, Parker, punctured his knee (that was not my proudest moment). But typically, I'm really good in a crisis.

If something is going on, or someone is suffering, hurting, or in need, I can get to the root of the basic needs and figure out a problem-solving solution in about three seconds. I'm a caretaker, and I'm a fixer, so my fixer side kicks in.

This really came in handy when I was taking care of my grandma so much a few years ago. If I had to go to the hospital with her for an emergency, the nurses, doctors, and CNAs always came in and commented on how well I handled situations. That didn't mean I didn't go into the bathroom after they left the room and have a complete breakdown. But I'm pretty good at keeping a level head, knowing what needs to be done, and getting it done at the moment.

Number 4 - I think out of the box.

That's *so* cliche, but it really is true. As far as real estate goes, there is no situation or problem that is not fixable. I truly believe that I've embodied that many, many times over my career. I'm able to communicate, especially to my clients, that *"This is a negotiation, and we're going to figure this out, and we're going to make it a win-win to get everybody to the finish line."* Several times I've brought things up when people have been at the end of their ropes and then are like, *"Ohhhhhhhh... I hadn't thought about that."* I have heard several times from my fellow agents, *"Oh, wait, that's a good idea."*

Thinking out of the box has helped me many times with difficult conversations, with an assignment that I maybe didn't understand, or, you know, outdated electrical secured to my home by duct tape, etc. It has definitely served me well in many situations.

So next - Number 5 - is that I have a super vivid imagination.

This one goes along with a couple of others, but the situation that sticks out to me the most happened in 9th grade. I had Ms. Harmon as my English teacher, and man, was she tough. You did NOT mess around in her class. We had this assignment where we were supposed to create our own Canterbury tale.

Procrastination can be — no, it IS - a sign of ADHD. And I have overcome this by always being early, giving myself false deadlines, etc…. but I was a procrastinator back then. *Big time.* Anyway, she was going to randomly call on people to get up and present our personal Canterbury tale. I was like, *"Oh, there are 25 of us in this class. What are the chances that I'm going to get called on the 1st day?"* So, we're sitting in class, and class hasn't started yet. We're all sitting around, and everybody's all nervous. And I'm like, *"I'm not nervous. I haven't even thought about what I'm going to say. But she's not going to call on me, so it doesn't matter."* Well, guess who got picked 1st? Whose name got pulled out of the hat very 1st? That would be yours truly.

I had not thought for the first second about what I would do for my story. Thankfully, I sat in the back row of the classroom, so I very, very slowly got up out of my chair and walked to the front of the room. It was probably just a second or two, but it was like on Seinfeld when Kramer goes into slow-mo, which is really normal for most...

So, I got up to the front of the class and stood at the podium. I had some public speaking experience, and I knew to get up there, take a deep breath, look around, make eye contact, etc. I probably bought myself five or six seconds. Truly, honestly, in those five to six seconds, I had the funniest story scenario occur to me, and I was able to tell my own Canterbury tale. I won't go into details as to what it was about, as it would be considered VERY un-PC these days, but it was funny.

When I started the story, I truly had no idea where it was going. I mean, I remember standing there in front of the class and thinking, *"OK, what comes next? What comes next? What comes next?"* And I would see an expression on somebody's face, or I would see a picture on somebody's shirt or something, and it would inspire me to carry on with the story and keep it going to the point that by the end, Ms. Harmon was sitting there crying from laughter because it was so funny. She was super straight-laced and conservative and still had to wipe her eyes with tissues from laughing so hard.

After class, I had a couple of classmates, one in particular, who were really mad at me. They were like, *"You can't tell me that you hadn't worked on that before today. There's no way you made that up on the fly. Blah, blah, blah."* Well, I did, and one of them STILL mentions that every time he sees me. He tells me I'm an impostor because he's just convinced that back in 9th grade when I said I hadn't prepared, I had. Whatevs (obviously, he needs something to do with his life). I walked up there and had the sickest feeling in my stomach. It was awful. But when I turned around and faced the classroom, it just started coming out, and I got an A. Anyway, that's an example of my crazy imagination, and it's definitely one of those that could work against me. I'll talk about some of those scenarios at another time. But yes, I have an incredibly vivid imagination.

On to Number 6 - I'm very empathetic.

And this, I'm finding, again, is very common among us ADHDers. We feel things very, very deeply, and we also are able to put ourselves in the shoes of the other person, sometimes to the point that it makes the situation even so much harder for us. I can usually see both sides of an argument, even if I don't agree with one of the sides. Even if I think one of the sides is nutso, I can still usually understand from where someone is coming...

This has definitely helped me as a real estate broker because it's helped me tell my clients, *"OK, let's put ourselves in their shoes. Let's look at their perspective. I don't think they're trying to be turkeys for turkeys' sake. I think they have a legitimate concern, you know, whatever, whatever, whatever."*

I definitely see this in both of my older children. In fact, they are probably *too* empathetic. Sometimes, if I'm upset or frustrated, they'll tell me to imagine I'm that person... *"How would you feel, Mama?"*

"Ugh. OK, yeah, you're right."

Number seven is HUGE - it's the hyper-focus.

I very obviously and very transparently struggle from moment to moment focusing on what I should be doing. I let squirrels distract me from my task at hand and that kind of thing. However, if I am against a deadline, or if I'm doing something that is super-duper important to a client, a family member, or somebody I care about, I go into hyper-focus mode. This will knock your socks off because the same stuff that distracted me 30 minutes ago can fly at me along with a tornado and a hurricane, and I will not be distracted from the task at hand.

This has definitely served me well. I can go back to high school and see times when I was able to pull all-nighters and not miss a beat at the moment. Of course, I would crash three days later, for, like, five days. But I've always been able to go when I really set my mind to something and hone in on the task or topic at hand. I struggle like crazy with run-of-mill day-to-day things, but when I am in hyper-focus mode, *watch out.*

I am proud of that one... until I rely on it. But that's another story!

Number eight branches from number 7 - I can display CRAZY stamina.

I get up really early in the morning, which is a conscious choice so that I get some quiet time before the rest of the house wakes up. Because of that, I go to bed super early at night. Like, don't call me after 8 P.M. I'm not going to answer. Shoot, don't call me after seven. I'm not going to answer. I am, without a doubt, no questions asked, going to be asleep.

When the time comes, though, I can really kick it. I can do a ten-hour road trip on just a couple of hours of sleep with zero issues. I might get to my destination and sleep for two days, but when I'm on the road, I am 100% OK, alert, ready to go, and cherishing the time. My stamina has benefitted me several times in my life, whether it's been when I needed to study for a test, drive to Pennsylvania to pick up a dog, or drive to the Outer Banks to teach a class... and then drive back the same day. I drove to Georgia and back in one day to pick up a video game for my son because the video game we ordered for him for Christmas didn't arrive in time. All in a day's work!

People think I'm nuts, but to me, it is just what you do when you have to do it. Granted, I was raised by a daddy who would drive to NY in one day to watch my brother pitch an inning and then drive home that same night... but now that I am older, I definitely see that most folks can't function that way!

Number nine - I'm funny without meaning to be.

I think number nine is just plain weird, but I hear it from enough people that I have to give it some legitimacy. People tell me all the time how funny and amusing I am and how I make them laugh. All I'm doing is just being me! I'm not putting forth the effort to be funny, and I'm not going into a situation saying, *"OK, I'm going to be funny right now."* It just happens.

I DO agree that I have facial expressions that are amusing. I see that a lot, especially on Zoom, and think, *"Wow, why am I making that face???"* I can also have... I don't want to say comebacks because that sounds sassy, but I can take a situation and put a positive spin or a funny perspective on it without really even thinking.

I know that sounds weird coming from me, but I hear it from people all the time. It kind of gives me the willies... almost braggy??... but if you know me, you know I am often truly shocked that people find me so funny.

Number ten - remembering random things through mnemonic devices and other weird tools.

I totally got this from my mama. I learned state capitals in 5th grade, and I still remember that the capital of Iowa is De Moines because I OWE YOU DA MONEY. She came up with crazy stuff to help me remember all of them. When I teach pre-licensing classes and when I am working with my kids on their homework, I come up with stuff that is just goofy to help them remember things. My kids would agree that sometimes Mama says things that are really odd, but they remember what they need to for the test!

This isn't exactly the same thing... I kind of lump these together... but I am really quick at putting things to song. I'm not saying that I always get the REAL lyrics right (right, Sherri?), but I definitely put things to a song in a way that I can remember them or make them memorable for others to fit a certain situation. For example, I remember when we announced one of our pregnancies to just a couple of really close friends (thankfully because it ended in miscarriage).

Anyway, at the time, Frozen was HUGE. I called one of my friends off the cuff and sang, *"Do you wanna hear a secret? You're gonna have a cow. I just took a test. It came back positive. I'm kind of freaking out."* It was off-key, but it was clearly *"Do You Wanna Build a Snowman?"* turned into a pregnancy announcement without any prep whatsoever. Even I realize most people don't do silly things like that off the cuff.

In high school and college both, if there was a particularly hard concept in math, history, or Latin that I couldn't remember, I would put it to music and make up a song about it. *Worked every time.* I've always said I wanted to write a children's book. I should do that. I should put that back on my list.

I've always had these weird ways of remembering things that strike other people as more work than they're worth. I'm very good at remembering numbers and random factoids. I've made up loads of songs over the years about family members and friends, sometimes to the tune of real songs. I did *"I Was Born a Coach's Daughter"* to *"Coal Miner's Daughter,"* and my version of *"Old Hippie"* nails Daddy and his wandering spirit. I can remember every phone number I had ever had - even back before we had to use the area code - and I can mimic every greeting my mama has ever left on her answering machine.

That's ten for now. There are definitely more, but I'm not going to just keep going and going and going. All of these, in some way, have served me well in my real estate career. They have served me well as a mama. They've served me as a wife. They've served me as a daughter, a caretaker, and a sister. So, I do really want to be sure to look at them as superpowers, as positives, and focus on them as gifts that I have thanks to this crazy ADHD diagnosis.

In short, if you ever need a new perspective... if you ever want a 30,000-foot view of a situation, just give me a call or text. I can usually give you a perspective that you haven't thought of before to make you feel better or at least make you laugh. That's part of the gift - I can take a situation and absolutely see the positive and see how to make it work.

So, if you're ever down or if you ever need a smile, reach out.

Chapter 4: The Dark Sides

I am a little unstable
Loose wires are always getting tangled now.
I am a little bit difficult.
I can be a little self-critical now.
I am a little unable.
To put all my cards on the table now
But somehow, You're still with me.

It's amazing that You can
Love me like I am

"Love Me Like I Am" For King & Country

So as much as I enjoy focusing on the optimistic side of things... I am the *"hashtag brightside girl"* ... there are definitely some downsides to ADHD. I don't want to dwell on those by any means, but I also think that those of us with ADHD deserve the validity of acknowledging that some parts of it, well... they just suck. *Period.*

I thought I would go along with my *"Ten Superpowers"* and simply give a flip side to those. I can't really organize these in that same way very well, so I'm just gonna jump right into them. One of the absolute *worst* things about my ADHD goes along fairly well with one of the positives. It's creativity. Creativity is wonderful in that I can make things up on the fly, be funny, and put a positive spin on hinky circumstances. However, this can also be a real negative.

Most commonly, I have seen this in my real estate career. Gary Keller himself wrote THE book on how to be a successful real estate agent. Many, many, many, many years ago, before Lisa and I were even at Keller Williams, she tried to get me to read THE book on running a successful business, *"The Millionaire Real Estate Agent."*

Besides the fact that I had some pretty strong feelings against some Keller Williams agents (those INTENSE feelings are another topic to be discussed shortly), I just didn't see the need to read the book. I was successful and making money, so why fix it if it isn't broken? Well, I wish I had fixed it because now, looking back, I can see that the models in that book would have made a tremendous difference in my business had I instituted them from the get-go. This would have, in turn, changed the entire trajectory of my family's legacy. Instead, I just flew by the seat of my pants for twenty-plus years, and I am just now starting to implement the models.

Those models are LIFE-CHANGING.

And when I say life-changing, I mean life-changing. They have made a tremendous difference in my business and my quality of life. However, I recognize that I still find myself at times wanting to put my own special touch on them...

New agents, do not do this! Are you listening????

These models exist for a reason; they are proven to work in various markets with all types of personalities. Admittedly, I still have to strongly fight the urge to put my own individuality on the models. Gary Keller will most probably never read this, but if he does, I want him to know that I know he's right. The models must come before creativity, and for me and other ADHD'ers, this can be a blessing; HOWEVER, in most scenarios, this is a curse.

Another thing related to creativity is my imagination. My imagination is usually pretty awesome. I can dream, and I can think of entertaining things that are motivating and inspiring. Sometimes, though, my imagination can get the better of me. Just ask Lisa.

We once had a client who was a dream seller. His home was pristine, and there was not a single thing out of place (Lisa already knows where this story is going...). Zero staging was needed. However, my biggest concern was that his home was TOO pristine and that folks would have a hard time imagining themselves there. He kept it in such great condition that it really was magazine worthy. And there was something about him that just didn't sit right with me. I was convinced - and you're going to spill your drink when you read this - but I was convinced he kept his wife in a box under the bed. Think about the *Law & Order SVU* episode with Andrew McCarthy. Andrew was a prince in *Pretty in Pink,* but MAN was he whacked in Season 1, Episode 22 of SVU! Squirrel...

Anyway, it didn't help that my seller's wife was Russian and a lot younger than he was (like in the SVU episode). I was absolutely convinced there was this sinister side to him. He was too neat and calm and controlling and way too smart for me to take him plainly at face value. Lisa laughs at me to this day.

The stories I made up in my mind about him! He was probably a great guy, and they probably had a perfectly happy marriage. His home was easy and breezy to sell, and he was a pleasure throughout the transaction. I CANNOT tell you, though, the number of times I got down on the floor and checked under his bed...

Because of that crazy strong intuition that I talked about in the previous chapter, I have a really hard time getting over my first feelings about people. If I meet someone for the first time and don't get a warm, fuzzy, comforting feeling, I automatically go into skeptical and suspicious mode. That has not served me well in a lot of instances.

Now don't get me wrong, it has been spot-on several times. As I said, I can't tell you the number of times Bradley has been amazed at how *"you called it, Precious."* But there are other times when I know, for a fact, I have not given people a fair shake simply because of a weird feeling. I can think of one instance in particular. It was another seller (no, not the one with the box under the bed...) whose company I DID NOT enjoy. All was OK until I saw her interact with her teenage kids. The hair on my neck stood up at how cold she was with them. I did not physically want to be around her from that moment.

I sold her home without a hitch, and we had a good working relationship. But I never let myself open up to her in the friendly way I do with most of my other clients. Ironically, she has been one of my greatest referral partners over the years. So, if she were really that bad a person, why would she continue to send business my way? I don't know, but I've often wondered if I missed out on a potential deep friendship there.

Oh, well.

So, let's talk about how I am in a crisis. While I am usually pretty good in a crisis *(other than that one time with my son's knee, anyway!),* being "good in a crisis" often manifests as wanting to take over and control things.

I remember when my mother-in-law died in a car accident. The siblings were all sitting around planning the funeral and what pictures they wanted to show. I wanted to take care of things so they wouldn't have to worry about it, so I voiced some very strong opinions. I ended up really ticking off some of them. They may not remember it, but I do, and I have always felt bad about that. My intentions were good; I simply wanted to get some things off their plates, but I was trying to take over like a bulldozer. Being good in a crisis can definitely manifest itself as being overbearing and too controlling, aka *"bossy."* I often ask myself, *"Amanda, do they REALLY want your help? Because if they don't, you're just making things worse."*

Procrastination - I talked in the last chapter about this one. My way of dealing with the natural procrastination of an ADHD'er is to overcompensate by being early.

Everywhere.

All. The. Time.

I can't tell you the number of times I have had people walk up to my car and ask if something's wrong. I cannot stand being late. Actually, I can't stand being right on time, either... but if I have a listing appointment or an appointment with a buyer, I will ALWAYS show up early and then have to drive around the neighborhood. I'm fairly certain it looks like I'm casing it. I don't want to pull into someone's driveway super early because they may not be ready for me. So, I'll either drive around the neighborhood or find a quiet cul-de-sac where I can park and wait. Well, I am convinced that more than once, people have thought I was a weirdo sitting there scoping out their kids.

68

As I said, it's not enough to be on time. I have to be early. Case in point: getting to church from our home takes about twenty minutes. I like to leave a good forty minutes ahead of time. It drives Bradley *crazy* - he wants to start getting ready about then. Ugh. What if we run into traffic? I can't stand walking in as the music starts. I want to be there with plenty of time to go to the bathroom, get my seat, and converse with my neighbors well before the service starts. I've always overcompensated for time. And that's definitely caused me to show up in some places inappropriately early. It's still better than being late, though. I don't care what anybody says.

Another one is hyper-focus. I can go into hyper-focus at work and get many things done in a substantially short amount of time. While that is excellent, I can also go into hyper-focus on something completely time-wasting and squander a whole day. I'm constantly dealing with little obsessions like Bogg bags, a certain author, or a certain type of dress or shirt. If I find something that suits me and is flattering, I will literally spend ALL DAY perusing the internet to find more, more, and more, and more. And one of every color. Black or navy? I want three of each! You can *never* have enough black or navy! The next thing I know, it's four o'clock, and I haven't gotten any lead gen done. The time literally dissolves like cotton candy in water when I'm like that. *It's crazy!*

Stamina is one too.

I've talked about the time that I rode to Georgia and back in a day to pick up a video game for my son. While that has definitely benefited me many times in my life, it's also resulted in me absolutely crashing for days at a time. In fact, it happened a few times when writing this book. I've sat down and started writing and just gone so long and deep into the night that my schedule has really gotten whacked out. I possess this intense dopamine-fueled energy that makes me an unstoppable, invincible superhero. Then a Hulk smash of fatigue wipes me completely out. There is no "in between," either.

There is also executive dysfunction. This is a fancy term for *CANNOT get your act together no matter how hard you try.* Unfortunately, the place where this has shown up most in my life is in our finances. If I had a dollar for every time I've paid an overdraft or late fee on something, we could buy a private island. Notice, I didn't say I needed the whole fee back - I just need a dollar *for every time it's happened.*

While I think Dave Ramsey is awesome, I'd also like to tell him to take a hike. When he says writing a bad check is a "lack of integrity," it absolutely is NOT always a lack of integrity. Sometimes it's merely forgetting to transfer funds, even though you wrote down two minutes ago that you needed to do that. Furthermore, it's thinking something is due on the 21st when instead, it was due on the 12th.

Regardless, an upset stomach, sleep loss, and everything else that comes with the territory of paying something late (or otherwise) show it isn't a lack of integrity! If integrity were lacking, we wouldn't give it a second thought. Seriously, though, I'm not knocking Dave. Not really, anyway. Wink wink.

The biggest evidence that this has been an issue for me is that I have had a garnishment and federal lien filed against my business. I can't believe I'm even admitting this. But hey, if it can help somebody, so be it. I wasn't a crook. I wasn't purposefully evading taxes. I wasn't purposely trying to hide anything or do anything wrong. It simply came down to the fact that my accountant, bless her soul, would send me paperwork to sign with instructions to sign and then mail to the IRS. I would open it and say, *"OK, I'll do this tomorrow morning first thing."*

Then by the time tomorrow morning first thing rolled around, it was underneath a pile on my desk. Then, six months later, when I decided to devote a day to organizing my office, I came back across it. In my eternal optimism, I would think, *"What is this? Oh, well, if this was important, Debbie would have taken care of it. Yeah. I'm pretty sure Debbie took care of it."* Well, guess what? Debbie had taken care of it by *sending it to me to take care of it.* But Debbie had not sent it in herself. This happened so many times that I ended up having a federal lien filed against me by the IRS. That's a fine one to explain to your bank when you're trying to do a refinance. (Thankfully, said federal lien has been paid, and I will keep the receipt forever and ever, amen).

OK, onto ANOTHER one... this kind of flies in the face of what I was saying earlier about being skeptical of people. But remember, I also said I go with my gut reaction, and this means I often see greatness in folks even when they don't see it themselves. Sometimes I can see TOO MUCH greatness (is that even a thing????).

Anyway, when I was the Productivity Coach in my real estate office, I came across many talented people with so much inside them. They just didn't think it of themselves. *"You can lead a horse to water, but you can't make it drink,"* - I would tell myself repeatedly. But every time one of them ended up leaving the business or leaving the company, I took it so hard because I saw it as a personal failure. I think some of them actually ended up going that route because of my belief in them - I blew them up so much because I saw so much talent and potential in them. When things didn't come naturally, it backfired. So yes, even with my overall skeptical nature, I definitely have a talent for seeing good in others. While on the surface, that's a good thing, it sure has caused me numerous sleepless nights.

I think the last one is just general inappropriateness. Most commonly, it is the fact that I'm funny without meaning to be. This can be a good thing, but sometimes I can say things that have me shaking my own head. I remember, in particular, a friend's wedding rehearsal. I was a bridesmaid, and I was so thrilled to be there. But I kept interrupting her and her hubby-to-be while they were trying to give their speeches. In my mind, I just wanted them to know *that I loved them, the wrapping paper was gorgeous, the whole setup for the rehearsal was beautiful, and tomorrow would be perfect and everything!* Looking back, I can see that I was completely inappropriate. I remember Bradley elbowing me a couple of times, and all he was doing was basically saying shut up. I kept spontaneously bursting out with things. They were compliments, but it had to have messed up their general flow of speech. Sorry, sweet Della.

Consequently, I can be in the middle of a very serious conversation. Someone can be talking to me about anything going on with them, even to the point that they are in tears, and at that moment, all they want is for someone to listen. In my brain, though, I am fighting with EVERYTHING I HAVE not to break into *Don't Take It Away* by Conway Twitty, *The Breakup Song* by Francesca Battistelli *("so FEAR, you will never be welcome herrrrreeeeee" complete with finger wag in the face),* or *Seven Year Ache* by Rosanne Cash complete with eyebrow flourish at *"God I hope he comes back soon."*

You get the point...

It's like there's this constant movie playing in my head that is putting images, sounds, and visions to whatever the person is telling me. It can also lend to the fact that I can have a ten-minute conversation with someone, walk away, and have no idea what we discussed. It isn't that I wasn't paying attention at first. Oh, I was paying SERIOUS attention, and then my imagination got the best of me, and I went off on some tangent, trying to solve the very problem you were just discussing. The whole time, I am nodding my head, saying yes, I get it, and things like that. It's incredibly frustrating sometimes and explains why I am a crazy notetaker with clients AND at church - if I take notes, I am focused and locked in 100%.

I can also be overly empathetic. I don't think empathy is bad, but when I take something so hard for someone else that it debilitates me, that is an issue. I also desperately want them to know that I understand what they are saying, so I will turn the conversation around to being about me. It isn't that I am selfish, want attention, or think my problems are worse than anyone else. It is just that I want them to know that I really do understand truly! I have to make a conscious effort to throw the ball back to them so they can resume their story.

I know for a fact that there have been several times when people have walked away from me when all they needed was a listening ear and felt like I was the most selfish, self-centered person in the world. That hurts my heart.

Then there is the energy. Sometimes my energy is so over the top that people think I am on drugs, which I find fairly amusing. Even in high school, I remember having a teacher question me and ask me once if I had been taking uppers. I was just hyper! I don't remember what I was specifically excited about, but I was so excited that I was giddy. I would talk fast, my hands would shake, and I would feel like I was about to burst with happiness. It TOTALLY came across like I had been smoking crack, and this still happens now. Try explaining that to a new class of aspiring real estate agents on the first day of class!

I also pick up on the energy of people in the room. I can walk into a meeting or class, intending to be an innocent bystander, a wallflower simply, and my energy will take over. I will then completely overwhelm the environment or situation. Think Kramer again. He bursts into a room and completely takes the focus off whatever is going on. He then leaves just as quickly, leaving everyone behind him wondering, *"What in the world just happened?"*

I actually DID get the Kramer award one year at work. I know Jill meant it as a positive because I am fun and spastic. I can throw a door open with the best of them. Right, Jilly?

And then there is the target on my back.

I DEFINITELY share this one with other ADHD'ers. We always think we are being watched. I can go to a ballgame and walk in the gym, and even though there are hundreds or thousands of people there, I feel like everyone here is looking at *me*... watching how I am walking... what I am wearing... how I am interacting with my kids...

It is like living with a constant spotlight shining on you. In reality, I know that nobody cares! Sure, they might see me, and I may get extra attention because I am super tall. I also have crazy gray hair that flies around all over the place, but people are not analyzing me. Neither are they talking about me nor worrying themselves over me as I feel. They just aren't. That's not normal, and even though my MIND knows that, my heart still can't help but feel like I am constantly being watched.

There's probably a little bit of paranoia mixed in there, too. I can remember, even as a young child, and even though my bedroom was on the second floor of our house, thinking people were looking in the windows at me. So, my PJs had to match, my room had to be neat, and my stuffed animals had to be lined up. What in the world is that???? People are way too busy with their own issues to worry about mine all the time. Like I said, I know that, but I still have a hard time shaking it sometimes.

I also feel things *deeply*. This is usually good in that it means I am empathetic and can offer a listening, caring ear to someone. However, it also means that I take things really hard. I will replay a conversation in my head for three whole days and think about how I should have handled it differently, perhaps, what I should have said differently... I will even come up with some amazing zingers and start praying that the conversation opens itself back up just so I can throw my zingers out there. I spend so much time taking things really hard and beating myself up. I probably could have changed the world for good in a substantial way in all the time that I wasted doing replays over the years.

And look, here I go again, being overly dramatic.

Imagine that.

I am sure there are others, and maybe I will get back to them at another time in this book. But a lot of mental and emotional energy is wasted due to my ADHD. And just because I know why now, it doesn't mean it isn't still exhausting. My mind is CONSTANTLY spinning, and while that is usually good, sometimes it can really take me down a dark path. Thankfully, I am close enough to the Lord to allow Him to snap me out of it after a time. I don't know what people would do without Jesus.

But that's a whole other book.

Chapter 5: Paradoxes

Sometimes I believe
That I can do anything.
Yet other times, I think
I've got nothing good to bring.
But you look at my heart, and you tell me
That I've got all you seek.

"Free to Be Me" Francesca Battistelli

When I was in law school, I had a friend named Christy. She and I, on the surface, were very different. One day she referred to me as a walking paradox because I was a *"Young Republican"* but also a *"heart on your sleeve liberal"* (her words). That title has always stuck with me, and now as I'm learning more and more about ADHD, I understand why we are, in fact, walking paradoxes (I so want to say paradoxi).

I can think of tons of examples. I hate mayonnaise, but I love ranch dressing. Who does that? Anyhow... there are several paradoxes that are pretty big in my life and have been pretty pervasive. So, I thought I would talk about those a little bit.

One of the biggest ones is our super sensitivity to noise. This is really big for me because I notice it at home. I notice it in the car. I notice it at work. I notice it at church. It's everywhere, and it's a paradox because things that I am super sensitive to other people may not even hear, and then other noises that irritate others, I find soothing. An example of this happened recently. I was in the car with my son Parker. We were on our way to church, and he had an empty Capri Sun. Y'all know those Capri Sun packages are the devil, right?

He would suck on it, blow it up, squeeze it, and then blow it up again. It was irritatingly random, inconsistent, and noisy. I finally just reached over and grabbed it out of his hands. He looked at me like I was crazy (all the while giggling), and I explained that the scratchy noise was driving me bonkers. He said (in his infinite wisdom), *"Mama, how do you hear all these little weird noises, but the sound of Tank (my very old but new to me vehicle at the time) doesn't bother you?"*

Admittedly, Tank is loud. I find it soothing, though, and I have even stopped listening to the radio riding down the road. The noise cocoons me like a white noise machine. But don't you dare let something random rattle in the console! I can't tell you the number of times I finally pulled over to find out *WHAT IS MAKING THAT NOISE!?!*

One night, I sort of had a flashback around this. I was lying on my bed going through some mail, and Parker and Elliott came in and started talking to me. Parker was getting ready to feed the puppies and had their metal bowls with him. He kept clanging them together, usually accidentally - but I was about to crawl out of my skin. I asked him twice to stop, and he did stop doing it intentionally, yet whenever he would move, they would make a soft ringing noise. I took it as long as I could and then basically hurled myself across the bed to grab them out of his hands (and pulled a muscle in the process). He and Elliott thought it was hysterical. Me? Not so much.

Back to the flashback. This got me thinking about a time in school when I probably should have gotten in trouble, but I didn't. In this case, the "girly" manifestations of ADHD probably saved my fanny. This story does go back to noise, so I promise I'll complete the circle in a second!

I had not thought of this in a really long time, but I used to sit on the front row in a certain classroom, and a boy that was in my same class for years sat behind me. He would tap, tap, tap his pencil on his desk constantly. It absolutely drove me insane, to the point that I asked to move several times. The teacher must have understood, because she would always let me move to the back of the room for at least a few minutes or until the next break.

Anyway, one day, she was out of class for a while, and even though I asked him nicely several times to stop, he kept tapping. I distinctly remember feeling like I was about to literally explode and finally turning around and slapping him across the face. I was such a rule follower - this was quite scandalous! I immediately started crying because I was afraid I would get in trouble. But when the teacher came back and found out what had happened, she looked at him and told him she hoped he had learned his lesson because she knew he had been getting on my nerves all year. She GOT me, and I'd love to tell her thank you.

Of course, now that I'm becoming more educated about ADHD, I realize he probably couldn't help it, either! What a great example of the differences between boys and girls. His hyperactivity versus my oversensitivity to noises. I won't say the grade because I don't want to give the boy's identity away, but this was at a pretty young age. I was also known as a crybaby at the time - I would get so frustrated and irritated that my emotions would bubble over.

It's kind of bizarre to look back and see how all of this makes total sense. Think about it - I was the tallest kid in class, yet I sat in the front row. I specifically remember asking many of my teachers at a very young age to please put me near the front. If I sit in the back, I get too distracted. Well, now I know why. I also prefer the front row at church, so sitting near the back where we currently go is *K-I-L-L-I-N-G* me.

I wish I had a dollar for every time *"Do y'all hear that?"* is asked in the Shore household. *"What is that? Seriously, you don't hear that????"* Even white noise is paradoxical for me. There are five white noise machines running in our house every night. I MUST have mine, but it can't be too loud. Bradley wants to crank the white noise up as loud as possible, and it's so loud it physically hurts me. He does not understand it and probably never will. Shoot, I don't either! I want it... but just a soothing touch.

Little things like clicking pins, oh my word, they drive me insane. The other night at church, there was a lady who kept saying, *"Amen."* Now, I have nothing against anyone getting into service. In fact, a lot of times, I'm probably the biggest offender of feeling the Spirit! But for some reason, on this night, I literally twitched every time she said it. Poor Bradley kept putting his hand on my leg because he knew it was getting to me. A few rows up from me, there was a young lady who I could tell was also being affected. I never did say anything to her, but I wanted to hug her neck and say, *Honey, we're gonna be okay.*

Another paradox is that we have to have everything out. We need things visible and accessible, or they don't exist. Seeing everything I'm possibly working on for the day out on my desk at work gives me a feeling of control, yet the clutter causes major anxiety. I get easily irritated, like major irritation, if I have to hunt for something, but I have so much out that I have to sift through it to find what I want, which irritates me further.

And it doesn't help that I'm visually motivated. I have pictures, motivational sayings, quotes - all kinds of things - posted around my desk. Seeing a particular picture can trigger a memory that sends me down a rabbit hole of distraction, but without the pictures and visual instructions to "think big, go small, trust the dominoes will fall" (thank you, The One Thing podcast!), I'll lose my motivation and be too overwhelmed to do anything. So, while I crave neatness and I crave order, the environment in which I am most productive from the outside is very messy.

People laugh at The Shore Team office at work because my business partner's desk is so neat with a cup of pens and a pile of papers and maybe one thing taped up on the wall, whereas my corner of the office is colors and pictures and motivational sayings and quotes and motivators and just all kinds of things to help me remember what to do. I mean, it really is pretty insane if you stand in the doorway and just look at my office. The problem is that if I don't have everything out, I'll leave something under a pile, and it'll sit there like a tax return and not get addressed. UGH.

Another paradox that kind of goes along with the noises deals with repetitive body-focused behaviors. So random noises drive me crazy, right? If you're sitting next to me and you pop your knuckles, I will go wide-eyed and every hair will stand on end. If I'm sitting at my desk and I hear someone an office over popping their fingers, or I hear their chair squeaking or something like that, it absolutely makes me lose my train of thought.

But I am the worst offender ever. I am constantly moving and shifting in my seat, so my chair is constantly creaking, and, oh, do I constantly pop my fingers, ankles, thumbs, and neck throughout the day! But there's a name for it! Repetitive Body Focus Behaviors are classic and common in ADHD'ers. They're related to self-grooming, anxiety management, and/or sensory stimulation. A common one is compulsive joint popping. And for me, it's my fingers and ankles... especially my ankles. If I don't pop my ankles regularly, and by regularly, I mean every couple of minutes, I feel like a volcano about to erupt.

In fact, one of the worst parts of my labor and delivery with my first son was that my epidural was too strong. At the moment, I thought this was a good thing because I didn't feel anything. But not being able to move my legs to pop my ankles was torture. I remember the middle of the night, May 7-8, 2009. My mama stood at the end of the hospital bed, lifting my feet up, trying to pop my ankles for me, and she just couldn't make them click. I got so irritated even though she was doing all she could.

Fortunately or unfortunately, there are others besides popping. A lot of them center around grooming, like hair pulling and playing. I play with my hair, which probably validates the "spacy" personality

ADHD'ers can seem to have – is there anything more stereotypically airheaded than a girl twirling her hair??? Anyway, as my hair has gotten longer, I have noticed that I am constantly twirling it and playing with it. And I used to fuss at my daughter so much for playing with her hair... oh well! The irony is that there is zero air in that head – it is FULL of thoughts and feelings.

My most obvious (and gross) one is skin-picking. The irony is that I do it the most when I'm in a happy, relaxed zone, like when I'm driving or when I'm at church. I don't do it at work. I don't do it when I'm sitting at the kitchen table with three little chicks and a yipping puppy. It usually happens when I'm relaxed. It would make more sense to me if it occurred when I was obviously stressed, like when I'm juggling 20 things at work. But it manifests mostly when I'm already doing something soothing, like driving (which I love!). I usually don't even realize I'm doing it - Bradley is all the time stopping me from messing with my fingers at church. Just the other night, I was taking notes and savoring my quiet time in church, but I ravaged my cuticles to the point of bleeding. Of course, once Bradley points it out, I feel the pain, but until he points it out, I can be ripping the skin away and not even realize I'm doing it.

Another paradox is that we often excel in our professions but are horrible money managers. We are typically extremely driven and entrepreneurial, and we excel in our chosen careers. But a common trait that I see is that we, and this definitely includes Amanda, are horrible money managers. I talked a little bit about this one earlier, but I'm going to go into more depth here.

This can show up in a lot of ways. We may have multiple income streams, and in our efforts to be a good steward, we set up separate accounts for different streams. But then this works against us because our eternal optimism and constant brain spinning prevent us from keeping what goes where and when straight. We often pay what's called the ADHD tax - late fees, forgetting to unsubscribe from things we don't use, struggling to return things in a timely fashion, and impulse spending.

The need to hoard favorite items is huge too. Why have one Bogg bag when you can have one in every color? Or you find a favorite lipstick color, then become convinced it's going to be discontinued, so you buy all six of the tubes in the store. Food expiring or going bad before we can get to it, paying excess shipping fees when we procrastinate on ordering things - there are so many ways this shows up!

We also have that blessed, infernal, eternal optimism. We fail to save as we should for a rainy day because the sun will eventually shine again even if it rains. It is a constant source of frustration. To know this is how my brain is wired, and not because I'm just a hot mess, is validating. And I can't tell you the relief I feel from knowing some of these things are not a lack of integrity (again, thanks Dave Ramsey); however, knowing it's how my brain is wired also tells me that I have a lot of important reprogramming to do, and that's a very intimidating thought.

And did I mention that we're often incredibly good handlers of other people's money? Our need to please and extreme concern for others often dictate that we're incredibly conscientious when placed in a supervisory role. For example, years ago, I was church treasurer and was very efficient, organized, and studious with every penny that came and went. But ask me to be that way with my own finances, and sadly, it's just not going to happen.

Another paradox that goes along with the one about craving order is that we can't close things to save our lives. I never close cabinet doors. Drawers are always left pulled halfway out. Twist tops are put on water bottles crooked, and notebooks and journals are never stored closed. I made a Facebook post at one point about sitting on my bed, and I could see the top drawer of my chest of drawers open, my closet doors ajar, a dress hanging on said ajar door half on a hanger and half off, a water bottle with the cap screwed on sideways on my nightstand, my bifold wallet lying open on my dresser, my favorite lipstick on my dresser without the cap on it, a pillowcase halfway on a pillow, and a suitcase on the floor, empty, yet open.

We are the very creators of the things that cause us difficulty! A neat and orderly room gives so much peace, yet we are our worst enemy in maintaining such. When I go into the office, I see the same thing. I try every afternoon to tidy up before I leave. But often in the mornings, when I walk in, I will see notebooks open with uncapped pens and piles of books lying sideways, about to topple over. When I went into the kitchen just this morning, I found the bottle of acetaminophen I used last night on the counter with the lid screwed on crooked, the water bottle I drank from to take it sitting uncapped with the cap right next to it, and the drawer from where I got the medicine pulled all the way out. UGH!!

Another paradox that is not so much a paradox is that we truly want to fade into the background. Well, I take that back - I guess it is a paradox. So often, because of our personalities and because of our lack of impulse control, we just can't do that. There were so many instances where I did not want a bit of attention. I wanted to fade into a wall and just observe, but then I became a focal point. A lot of that comes from the fact that we just feel things so big, whether it's happiness, sadness, or anger... our brains don't regulate our feelings, so we don't react the way most do. I can see this helping explain why so many of us females with ADHD are diagnosed with bipolar disorder and other mood disorders.

We have rejection sensitivity dysphoria and other aspects of ADHD that have given me so much clarity into certain things that have happened in my life. For example, when I was five or six and eating at Shoney's with my family and my grandma, I got tickled at something and couldn't stop laughing. This may not sound like a big deal, but in my family, the children sat at the table and were quiet, ate their food, and let the adults talk. But this particular time, I couldn't stop laughing. This went on for what felt like ages. I truly couldn't stop, no matter how hard I tried, to the point I was crying, not happy tears but *"Why can't I stop laughing?"* and *"What is wrong with me?"* tears because I was embarrassing my family and drawing attention to our table. This was a hard moment for someone with a stronger than most urge to be a people pleaser. An older gentleman even walked by our table, tapped me on the shoulder, and said, "Cheer up." To this day, every single time I drive past that old Shoney's location, I cringe.

Another time that I really wanted to fade into the background was in high school. Pretty much throughout high school, I wanted to be persona non grata. But as I wrote earlier, I was a teacher's kid. I was an athlete, I was all these things that really contributed to being unable to quietly fade. I even ran for Student Body President because it was expected of me. I don't regret that now looking back, but man, was I miserable, and how hard I prayed someone else would run so I would be opposed. The target on my back was so big already!

Let me give you an example of what I mean about the target. One day the drug dogs were brought to our high school. Remember, great athlete, Student Body President, teacher's kid...I always felt like I was being watched. Anyway, I remember standing at the classroom window that overlooked the parking lot and seeing the principal direct the dogs down the road where my car sat. I had a beautiful, perfect, gorgeous grey Lebaron convertible; that car was my life. But I digress. They got to the end of the row and circled back to my car. And did that again. And again. It turned out that the car next to mine was full of weed and paraphernalia. A friend looked at me and said, *"Oh my gosh. I thought they were double searching your car."* When she said that, I lost it. How dare they single out my car? (They were not doing that). How dare they make me an example? (They were not doing that). The next morning, I went straight to the principal's office and burned a lot of bridges with a man who had always been a tremendous advocate.

Man, it's sad to think back on but so indicative of how several things in high school went down. I so wanted to fade into the background, but because I felt things stronger than most - good and bad - that was simply impossible. That's probably also why I don't look back on high school with joy. AT ALL. Zero.

When I was a senior at Carolina (THE Carolina, as in UNC), I was president of a co-ed honor fraternity. That fraternity was my life for four years. We studied hard and played hard. One night at a party, the girlfriend of a good friend of mine commented that she always knew he - and "he" shall remain nameless - would be taken care of during the week because of our friendship. She probably meant it sincerely and in a good way. But my reaction was over the top. I won't go into the detail simply to save myself the embarrassment, but man, did I show my tail! She was simply trying to give me a compliment, and I completely lost my mind. I even resigned as president and left the fraternity the very next day. I felt I had disappointed everyone so deeply that I completely walked away from the best part of my time in college. And I will always regret that.

When Bradley and I first married, we lived next to a precious couple on the river. They loved us and watched over us without being intrusive. They let us do our thing, did their thing, and were just wonderful. They also loved our dogs like crazy. One day, I came home to a message on the answering machine from Sandra. She was upset because my Butter, the best dog EVER, had killed one of her kittens. I'm leaving out a lot of details, but to make a long story short, I headed out the door, marched across my yard and then hers, and blessed her out. I decided that day that we were moving. And guess what we did? Within a week, we had packed up and moved into my mama's old house over a silly phone call.

So much for fading into the background! There are so many examples of this kind of thing - extreme elation over the good and extreme disappointment over the bad, especially when I felt questioned or rejected or felt a loved one was being questioned or rejected. The irony of it is that oftentimes when I was in social situations, I would intentionally fade into the background and stick myself in a corner... yet I would feel rejection and disappointment when people did not seek me out. Weird, right?

I've lamented often that I thought that as we got older, we were to care less about what people think. Instead, it seems I care more every day than I did the day before. If I know you, I love you so big. Conversely, if I feel rejected, I will cut you off completely in a hot second. This has caused me to have very few long-standing deep relationships (if you are one who has weathered the storm, I salute you and love you dearly!). Knowing this about myself makes me super aware of my reactions - I am thankful for this knowledge, but I'm hesitant to celebrate. Just knowing why I'm like this doesn't change the roadmap of my brain. I pray I can use this new awareness for good.

So, if you see these things in your kids...I'm not asking you to excuse their behaviors and reactions, but maybe take a step back and put yourself in their shoes. Imagine feeling something deeply while simultaneously thinking, *"You're nuts."* Feeling it so deeply and being unable to change how you feel is beyond mentally exhausting.

Now, imagine you also feel you're letting down everyone around you. It's brutal. For a 48-year-old woman with awareness, it's crippling. So just imagine how it feels to a CHILD.

There's a popular meme on Facebook. Actually, it's a series of memes that goes along with these paradox conversations. We're mentally, emotionally, physically drained, and disorganized. The exhaustion, constant anxiety, and overwhelm are debilitating. Yet we're pleasers and perfectionists. We're creative problem solvers...we stress incredibly hard to make things work, so we can avoid feeling like a failure. Yet we experience criticism more painfully because we try hard to throw everything into the bucket. No matter how hard we try, we can't do everything right. So, then we feel criticized even more. In reality, people think we are rock stars, so then we feel like phonies.

It's just a constant cycle. We are constantly overwhelmed trying to manage the details of everyday life. And then we spend all night beating ourselves up because we didn't do the details right when, in reality, we probably did more than anyone else.

It's hard to explain, but you'll understand if you've been there.

Chapter 6: Science

I am a little uneven
In need of a little more healing now.
Yes, I am!
And I feel a little unfixable.
You're nothing short of a miracle now.
'Cause somehow, You're still with me

It's amazing that You can
Love me like I am

"Love Me Like I Am" For King & Country

So now I'm going to get a little scientific... well, as scientific as I can get.

I watched a documentary on ADHD with my husband recently. He has lived with my spinning brain for 23 years now, and he has a degree in psychology, so if anyone would see the legitimacy of this diagnosis, he would.

It started as a simple documentation of watching someone with ADHD eat lunch. You know, how they would start fixing their lunch, and then they would notice that they needed to take the trash out, and then when they went to take the trash out, they would notice that the cat needed to be fed, then they would eventually make it back into the kitchen to finish fixing their lunch, but they would forget what they were fixing and so on and so on and so on. Then, once they sat down to eat, they would not want what they had fixed because they were no longer hungry. So, they would throw away part of their trash, but not all of it, and leave the trash can lid open... all the while loading the dishwasher and running a load of laundry.

He watched it and kind of dismissed it (though not in an ugly way). When I said, *"You realize that's exactly how I've lived for over 47 years now,"* he seemed genuinely surprised. He said, *"Really?"* with about 15 exclamation marks and question marks. We talked for a few minutes, comparing how his thoughts were so different than mine. He then went on to say, *"No wonder you're so tired at night. It's like you've been running sprints all day."*

Bingo.

So, if my master's-degree-in-psychology-toting-firsthand-account-eyewitness doesn't realize this is a true representation, I can understand why people are so intrigued by the ADHD discussion. Speaking of my poor husband, he has had to deal for over 20 years with random fixations - 18 Bogg bags, being easily triggered, random energy bursts that often happen very early in the morning, tons of alone time needed, not wanting to be touched... and when your husband's number one love language is physical touch, just imagine how that makes him feel! And then new hobbies and ideas allllll the time.

So, as I said, I want to be a little bit scientific-y. Is that a word? Trust me, it won't be very scientific because that's not how my brain works. But I would like to address a term called executive dysfunction. This one really gets me going because a lot of people think that our executive dysfunction is limited to things that we don't like... like cleaning the house or school work or paying bills and things like that. But I think of all the times I've been meaning to plug my phone in, and I've gone from 32% to 2% because I've been engrossed in something, and an hour has gone by completely unaware. THAT is walking, talking executive dysfunction.

Executive dysfunction is not laziness or procrastination. Laziness is when you don't want to do a task and <u>choose</u> not to do it - and you're fine with that. You don't care if it gets done, and you don't worry. You figure someone else will do it. Procrastination is when you want to do the task but put it off because it seems difficult, boring, or time-consuming. Executive dysfunction is when you want to do the task, and you intend to do the task, and there's no significant reason not to do the task, but you can't because your brain is having difficulty transitioning between activities *(and writing complete sentences apparently, right?).*

Executive function is how we manage ourselves and our resources in

97

order to achieve a goal. It's mental control, and self-regulation, an umbrella term for our daily conduct. So, in short, executive DYSfunction means everyday life is a bit harder to manage. This is true in women, especially because our tendency to overcompensate makes us look like we're the most together when, in fact, the inner workings of our brains look like a train wreck. It's much harder for us to get from point A to point B.

To so many people, executive dysfunction is all about organization, but it isn't just organization.

It's initiation. We struggle to start tasks, as we always think something else needs to happen. For example, before I can clean out a closet, I have to figure out what I'm going to do with the extra stuff. Do I want to donate, sell, or trash? If I sell, do I do it on Facebook or Poshmark? And before I do that, I have to see how much trash I already have for the week. I have too much already, so I can't do ANYTHING until trash day. So, it sits in various piles throughout the house for six months.

It's inhibition. Once we do start, we struggle to stop. There is a lack of impulse control. We don't clean often, but when we do, nothing is safe, and we're going *alllllll* day. That pile that has been there for six months? Watch out, 'cause when I am in the vibe, it is G.O.N.E.

It's emotional control. We have a hard time managing our reactions. We take things harder or more personally than most, and we're

98

unreasonably excited about something that isn't a big deal to most. *Yes!!! Dimmers in the new office!!! Let's party!* OR, *Oh no!!! He didn't write me a review – he must've thought I was awful!*

It's shifting. We have a hard time transitioning from one task to another. Like, I must finish this before I start something else because if I do, I won't do it *per-fect-ly.* So, since we have trouble finishing things and being satisfied enough to call it quits, nothing gets done.

It's working memory. We struggle to communicate things to others. Even though something we heard greatly impacted us, the thought flees. This often shows as struggling to explain an idea I heard in a class to a coworker that I felt could be life-changing when I heard it... *but then I can't put it into words to save my life.*

It's planning and organization, the ability to manage current and future tasks, like having big dreams yet having no idea where to start to accomplish them, and big ideas that are wonderful and will bring so much joy to so many people. But just getting started with the simple steps is impossible. I have been dreaming of writing a "real book" since I was about 10... and here I am, 37 years later...

It's organizing materials and keeping things in order so they're easily retrievable. We need it visible to be relevant. As I said, we keep our work and personal receipts together because even having one place for all receipts is incredibly challenging, but having them together creates more problems down the road. *Was that a charity purchase or a business expense? Was that a payment plan payment, and I have already deducted the full amount, or am I double dipping?*

Executive dysfunction is how we monitor and manage ourselves around others. We interrupt, or we tune out. We seem rude when we build our bunker so we can focus, and other times, we gush. We just overreact in so many different ways. No matter what way, though, it's *extra*.

So many common ADHD memes showcase a messy home or a messy car; however, executive dysfunction isn't just about being messy or having dirty dishes in the sink. It's open drawers, cabinets, and a dishwasher hanging open and smelling up the kitchen. Bradley always used to ask why I couldn't close things or put lids on straight. Well, our brains tell us to get the plate out of the cabinet, and as we walk over to the cabinet to get it out, it's already telling us to do 18 other things. So, the fact that we get the plate out of the cabinet is a miracle because as we're reaching for the plate, we're turning to do something else already, and closing the cabinet door isn't even on the list. It isn't just that we are "disorganized" but that we have 47 pistons firing at once.

One of the ways that executive dysfunction is so problematic is that

AHDers often mask it in ways that make us seem super competent. We often have a high IQ. We perform well in school because we have an inherent expectation of success, but we're even more confused and ashamed of our difficulties and driven to hide our struggles. We compensate for our challenges... and then become obsessive about organization and structure, leading to intense anxiety, which leads to burden and exhaustion.

Do you see how it's just a constant circle?

As neurodivergent women (especially), we often slip through the cracks because we appear so smart and gifted, are more likely to be perfectionists, and suffer from low self-esteem. So, what do we do? We work extra hard to prove ourselves, and then we end up burning out. Combine that with hyperfocus, where one thing can hold our attention for hours, and we appear brilliant.

I read one book where we were called "The Lost Girls," and as sad as that made me, I absolutely loved it. We are either superheroes or super failures, and it isn't our lack of interest that makes it hard for us to process things. It's that our brains desire to absorb it and to do it perfectly. We all have missed red flags that haunt us. I mentioned how the masking of our executive dysfunction could translate into seeming to be brilliant - and there probably is some brilliance there - but I had a funny conversation with a former coworker recently.

Before I was a real estate agent, I was a juvenile court counselor, which is a fancy name for a probation officer. This was back before email and fancy computers. We kept everything together on paper and in binders, and this former coworker took over part of my caseload when I left the job to go into real estate. She said she sat down with my binder, ready to call some kids, and there were no phone numbers anywhere.

She thought, surely, there are not this many kids that don't have home phones. So, she called me, and I said, *"Oh, what number do you need?"* And then I just rattled off all the numbers to her. She asked why I didn't have the numbers in my book, and I said, *"Oh, I just have them memorized."* I had over 50 kids on my caseload! But then she also saw in my book notes where I would go to the wrong house because I would juxtapose the numbers in the address. So that brilliance also went right alongside the perception of the nutty or the absent-minded professor.

I was talking to a current coworker recently, and she was convinced that her husband has undiagnosed ADHD. There were some interesting realizations that came from our conversation. For example, if your ADHD spouse isn't a list maker, don't ask them to make a list to be more productive. One of my coping strategies over the years, even though I did not know it was a coping strategy, has been excessive list-creating. But if it doesn't originate with me, I'm helpless. If someone else asks me to make a list, that's just adding another "to-do" to my brain. So, for someone who hasn't mastered list making, telling them to make a list to get things done is like asking them to grab all the dollar bills in the money machine thing at Chucky Cheese.

My suggestion to her was to make a list for him. Then he will have a place to start, and he doesn't have to go into overdrive on organization, prioritizing, and detail remembering. I then told her she should really be talking to my saintly husband or my beyond-patient and grace-giving business partner, Lisa. They are the real MVPs!

I also told her that if you're scheduling something for him, and he says it will take an hour, block two hours for it. Give him grace to go over the expected time because we definitely think we can get more done than we can in an allotted time. Then, if we finish early, we can let our extremely tired, fatigued, motorized brains rest.

She said to me at first, *"But he isn't hyper."* BINGO! It isn't necessarily that our bodies are hyper. When I get excited, I'll talk 3000 miles an hour and get louder and louder. But our brains... that's why we go from energy through the roof to asleep in three minutes. Our brains go and go and go like a hamster in a wheel for hours with no break. It's exhausting. Then when we stop, we're done.

I have beaten myself up so many times over the years for feeling ungrateful, tired, and overwhelmed - especially when it comes to parenting. My husband and I struggled with infertility for years. We had two precious children, we had two miscarriages, and then we had our third. We prayed, and we prayed, and we prayed and spent thousands of dollars for exactly what we have.

So, shouldn't I be soaking up every minute of it?

What's wrong with me that my greatest blessings are sometimes too much, and I have to just go away?

Why do I need more quiet time than most when I have exactly what I beseeched God for all those years?

I know all mamas get tired, and I know all mamas get overwhelmed, but I don't think they get to the point that they must take a break for a bit as often as I do to save their sanity. I've often said the Lord gave me a husband with a psychology degree for a reason, and this is definitely one. Bradley may not always get it, but he always gets ME and lets me have that time. So, finding out that I'm not just ungrateful, I'm not lacking a mama gene, I'm not hateful, and nothing is wrong with my heart is a huge relief. It's me. It's how I'm wired. My bucket can get overloaded with any kind of chaos, even the best kind, and demand that I have a break. I'd give anything to go back and relive all the *"Here I sit with so much more than I deserve, so what is wrong with me?"* moments. I can't do that, but I can recognize moving forward that I simply need my sensory bucket emptied. There is nothing wrong with me. I am not a bad mama. I am not a horrible, ungrateful person.

I still feel guilty at times. That's another lovely trait of us ADHD'ers - we question ourselves more than most and are harder on ourselves than most. Now, though, I recognize when it's happening and give myself more little breaks to ward off some of the need for big ones possibly. That way, my kids get the mama they deserve more consistently. They deserve the best because they are the best.

This isn't very science-y, is it? So, onward!

I get asked a lot about medication. When I was first diagnosed, I went to therapy. As I gained a greater realization of this diagnosis, my doctor and I decided medication may be beneficial. It wasn't like I could go to bed at night and say, *"Oh, tomorrow will be a better day,"* like I had always done. I now went to bed thinking, *"Oh my word, this is how my brain is built, and there's nothing I can do about it."*

So, at one point, I started meds and didn't stick with it. I loved that I was less of a "walking disaster area," per my mama, but I also felt like I lost a little spring in my step. I liked being able to function and focus. I liked walking through the kitchen and not having a single cabinet door open. I liked dropping the kids off at school and my stomach not being in knots because I felt like I was behind schedule getting to work. I liked picking the kids up and not pulling into the parking lot with an empty gas tank on two wheels. And when Worth, aka Hulk, was watching Curious George, being a superhero, coloring me a picture, and playing with Bluey and Friends, I didn't get overstimulated. I just smiled and soaked it up.

So, I saw good things in the medication. I just didn't feel like myself. I didn't make random analogies that cracked people up. I didn't walk into a room like Kramer and offer irrelevant opinions. I didn't feel the high highs after talking to a content client. I taught classes and stayed seated the whole time instead of pacing, hopping around, and gesturing so much that I popped my shoulder out of the socket.

I was present, and I was happy. But I wasn't ME.

I felt like I was watching the world go by rather than being fully involved in it. I would drive Elliott to dance and not break into random, made-up song lyrics. She probably loved it, but to me, it was sad. I didn't like that when I would cook a meal, I would think ahead and fix so much that we would have leftovers for days - because then I didn't get the chance to come up with some bizarre yet delicious concoction of foods that my Parker absolutely loved that were never meant to be combined.

I just felt DIM. I didn't feel like my light was shining brightly, and I didn't like it. I was functioning and focusing, but I was not flourishing. *Flourishes are what make life interesting, aren't they?*

It was an interesting little jaunt into the medication world. I remember one day telling a friend that I couldn't tell the difference, and I was surprised since I had been on the meds for a few weeks. But then the next day, I realized that I had come home from work, fixed the kids' supper in 15 minutes, folded laundry as soon as it finished drying, and loaded the dishwasher immediately following supper. I left work with plenty of time to get gas and still picked up Worth with minutes to spare.

So, the medication was definitely *definitely* making a difference. But then, when I wanted to talk to my doctor about it, as wonderful as she was, I had such a hard time articulating what I meant. I never got the run-around, don't get me wrong. But women so often do, and that's why we're misdiagnosed and misunderstood. Boys are four times more likely to be diagnosed with ADHD than girls because of how the symptoms manifest.

So high-functioning women who are miserable, who realize they're miserable, who don't want to be miserable, who beat themselves up because they're miserable, don't receive the validation that they should from the medical community. ADHD is missed in women because it looks different. We are constantly overwhelmed trying to manage the details of everyday life, and we're likely to zone out even in the middle of an important conversation. We're working really hard to try to manage our thoughts.

It's like we're balancing 15 balls full of toxic chemicals, and if we get all the balls to the finish line, everyone will get a million dollars, but if we drop even one, everyone will die. So, the stakes are super high either way. There's mental, emotional, and physical disorganization, but the depression and anxiety resulting from those things are usually what is treated.

It's exhaustion, constant anxiety, and overwhelm. We feel everything all the time. We're often people pleasers, perfectionists, and creative problem solvers who find ways to get by. But we stress so hard, and then we will do anything to avoid feeling like a failure. We cover our symptoms in ways that look like obsessive-compulsive disorder. So, because I left my stove on once before I left the house, I now compulsively check my stove. Because I have gotten to a ballgame before with no sunglasses, I have 18 pairs in different spots (but none in the car I'm in at the moment).

We're really good at masking our symptoms. We judge our difficulties as personal flaws, and we are very good at hiding our ADHD challenges from others. We hyper-focus on things we're really interested in. We procrastinate a lot. We wait until the last minute to start important work because we have to feel the pressure to get it done in a frenzy. We spend hours doing it the night before, yet we also want it to look like we spent weeks working on it.

Somehow, somewhere we are messy. If you follow me on Facebook, you know my messy place is my house. I may look presentable with a matching outfit or a reasonably organized desk at work, but my house is a disaster. My car is even worse. My coworkers come out to my car with me and have to dodge the three coffee mugs and two bags of trash that spill out as soon as I open the door.

We constantly worry about forgetting things, or we actually forget them. We always feel like something has fallen through the cracks. And when we're trying to focus on a conversation, it's like people are constantly interrupting, but the other person doesn't know and doesn't hear the interruptions. So, then we hyper-focus so that we can really pay attention, and then that sends us off on the daydream trail. We'll "zone out" even in the middle of an important conversation.

Some people really think women can't have ADHD. They think you can't have it if you're smart or did well in school. Well, guess what? A lot of times, those things are the very indicators of it.

And we are exhausted.

Chapter 7: Executive Dysfunction Hacks

I keep fighting voices in my mind that say I'm not enough.
Every single lie that tells me I will never measure up.

Am I more than just the sum of every high and every low?
Remind me once again just who I am because I need to know.

You say I am loved when I can't feel a thing.
You say I am strong when I think I am weak.
And you say I am held when I am falling short.
And when I don't belong, oh, You say I am Yours.

"You Say" Lauren Daigle

Remember the Amen lady?? I tried really, *really* hard not to let my head turn every single time she said it. I did not want to be a distraction myself, and I surely didn't want to get my kids' attention off what the preacher was saying. Every time she would say it, I would make a hash mark on my notepad *(I have to take notes to stay focused, remember?)*. My therapist taught me this little trick to get over the distraction quickly. Instead of expending my energy being frustrated and bracing myself for when the next one will come, I draw a hash mark. That way, it's over and done. Time to move on!

I talked in the last chapter about executive dysfunction and how our brains are made in such a way that things are simply harder for us to accomplish. One of the things that I've done my whole life is come up with little tricks like the hashmark one to help myself. I never knew it was because I had ADHD, but I always knew I needed additional things in place to help me accomplish the things that seem to come to other people easily. As an ADHD'er who loves lists, I made a couple for this book!

Number one: Utilize alarms and reminders to the nth degree. I literally have "Worth's clothes" set as a reminder every Monday through Friday at 06:15 A.M. as I will not remember to get his clothes out if I don't. Yes, even though I do it every day! And be choosy with audio alarms. I always have my phone on silent because every text tone, ring, etc., messes with my groove. With my phone on silent, I know to check my calendar often (see number three coming up). I have a time block for returning texts and phone calls (see number eight). Otherwise, there would be no way I could get anything accomplished.

Number two: Always ask for written instructions and always write your own instructions. We will get numbers, dates, and times mixed up within five seconds of being told. If a meeting is from 10 to 12 on the 2nd, it's too easy to show up at 12 expecting a meeting until two on the 10th. And if there are more than two steps, this is even more critical. My big-picture brain loves to run to the finish line without properly jumping over the hurdles. I'm like a goofy Great Dane puppy running right through them, wreaking havoc and destruction. I still get to my destination, but it's usually not pretty, so having a written reference is mandatory. This also keeps me from relaying instructions incorrectly. Telling your partner to go to 323 Main Street when it's really 332 Main Street is not cool, especially when she ends up on the wrong back porch scrounging around the grill looking for a key. Sorry, sweet Lisa...

Number three: Make a schedule and insure you can check it multiple times a day. Written planners work for some, but I'm a Google calendar girl. I always have my phone with me, and I can and do check my schedule constantly. It's also color-coded, so I know if pink shows up, it's Elliott, blue for Parker, red for Worth, etc. If I see pink or blue during the workday, something very out of the norm is happening (remember, a lot of us are very visual). I have reminders for everything - including *"go to the bathroom"* because if I don't, I'll wait too long and barely make it. *Daily. Multiple times a day.*

Number four: Break down large tasks into small ones. I struggle with this one daily. I often don't start something because I won't be able to finish it. And if you're going to do something, do it right, right? I have to really reprogram myself to do something right <u>at that moment</u>. I preach to our new agents, *"Think big, go small, trust the dominoes will* *fall"* (thank you again, The One Thing podcast!), yet this eludes me at home. Last weekend, I organized one bathroom drawer, and that was a huge accomplishment, as I've been putting off bathroom reorganization for over a year now due to not having enough time to do it all.

Number five: Keep your work and play areas completely separate. Even at home, I have a tightly defined designated work space. Ideally, though, I'm in the office if I'm working. My brain needs my home to be my safe haven and my work to be where I get stuff done. Bradley can sit on the couch with his laptop and be incredibly productive, even while watching Doctor Phil. It's mind-blowing to me.

Number six: Set reminders to let you know when transitions are coming. If I'm working on my database, I set the alarm to remind me at 9:45 and 9:55 that I have a 10:00 A.M. appointment. Otherwise, I'll hyper-focus and work right through it. I also set alarms for everyday basic stuff. If I need gas on the way home, I'll set one that morning so I know not to work until the last second. Then I don't have to drive to my destination on fumes because I didn't have time to stop for gas. External reminders are great too. I'll call my assistant and ask her to write a note and stick it on my keyboard, and she still knows to check it an hour later to make sure I've done it. Bless her.

Number seven: Take breaks from interacting. Yes, yes, and TRIPLE YES.

I take field trips on days I'm in the office. It may be just for 10 min, but a quick drive from Silas Creek up Business 40 to the other end of Stratford does my body good. I also have a *Do Not Disturb* sign on my door at work. A coworker wrote "Why?" beside it last week. Not that I should have to explain, thank you very much, but I'm often zooming with clients and need privacy. And number two, sometimes I simply need uninterrupted quiet time. It's hard to explain, but you'll understand if you've experienced it. Sometimes, if I have to have one more conversation, I will explode and not with anger. It isn't that I don't love people - it's more like a sensory overload. I can literally feel my skin heating up and my hair standing on end like I'm wound up tight as a buzzer. If I say I need alone time, I NEED alone time.

Number eight: Set expectations with those in your world. I don't always do a great job at this, but I always try to let my clients know that my rough schedule is database in the morning, paperwork and firefighting midday, and appointments in the afternoon, so a text from 8:30 to 11 may not get an immediate response. My poor friends also know we may be in the middle of a conversation, and I may drop off the face of the earth for four days, and then I'll pick right back up as if I never left them hanging. I know Megan is giggling (or maybe rolling her eyes?) right now as she reads this. My team members know to put me on silent because if I have a random thought at 4:30 in the morning, I will communicate immediately by text or email. If I don't send it when I think it, it's gone with the wind.

Number nine: Put white space in your schedule. If I think an appointment's going to be 30 to 45 minutes, I will block an hour. Otherwise, I'm running behind everywhere I go. And I *DETEST* being late. In fact, to me, being on time is being late. It makes me nauseous. I can't tell you the number of times this has saved my schedule. I also realize being early can sometimes seem rude. Numerous times over the years, I've parked down the street of a home where I had an appointment. I talked about that in another chapter. I've met some wonderful neighbors that way... wink wink...

Number ten: Recognize that you're wired this way, and no matter how great your intentions are, you must utilize some hacks if you want to feel accomplished, respect others' time, and in general feel like a good and productive human. Remember, we are harder on ourselves than most. So, when I'm five minutes late, I feel like I've let my people down in a big way. A little or a lot of pre-planning goes a long way. I've learned that my natural tendency is to triple-book myself and that it isn't going to change. So, intentionality around building in breaks and white space is essential for myself and all of humanity.

The irony of all this is that I'm considered highly social, and in an industry where conversations and interactions are critical, I think my

40-minute commute is my saving grace. On the way in, I have time to get my mind right, and on the way home, I have time to decompress. I'm usually able to present my optimistic, upbeat self because I intentionally withdraw periodically. If I don't, I feel like an electrocuted cat looks - my sensory bucket overloads, and I start talking crazy fast, my eyes tear up, I get irritable, snippy, and jittery, and that's not who I want to be.

Thank God, I now know these things happen for a biological reason and not just because I'm a whack job.

Chapter 8: All the Things

You mend what once was shattered.
And You turn my tears to laughter.
Your forgiveness is my fortress.
Oh, Your mercy is relentless.

My help comes from You.
You're right here, pulling me through.
You carry my weakness, my sickness, my brokenness
All on Your shoulders
Your shoulders

"Shoulders" For King and Country

So, this last chapter has been a long time coming when looking at the timeline of compiling this book.

I've struggled with the organization (duh). I've sat down to do it 20 times, gotten overwhelmed, and said *I'll do it later.* Finally, my sweet husband remarked, *"Babe, the whole book is about ADHD. Isn't it appropriate for the last chapter to be random?"*

Bless his heart.

So yes, this chapter is very random, even more random than the rest of the book, as it's just lots of little snippets and thoughts that I've had and learned that I think are important and should be included. And, of course, it will end with some list-making.

Did you know that dental issues are related to ADHD? There are so many things - oh gosh, there are so many things - that looking back on my life, I can see, oh, now I know why that was the way it was! And dental issues are one of those. There's an awesome podcast by Tracey Otsuka that talks about it, and I would definitely recommend it. How random, right???

What people think ADHD is and what it really is, in reality, are so very different. I saw a meme that shows the tip of the iceberg with the words "having trouble focusing" and "fidgeting." But then, under the surface of the water, there's this list of things like difficulty maintaining relationships, depression, difficulty following and maintaining conversations, inability to focus even if there are no distractions, executive dysfunction, poor impulse control, forgetting to eat, sleep, go to the bathroom, problems focusing on things even if they are of interest, choice paralysis, difficulty switching tasks or inability to stick to one, losing items relentlessly, chronic unemployment, forgetting thoughts two seconds after having them, rejective sensitive dysphoria, trouble regulating emotions, auditory processing disorder, sleeping problems, trouble recalling commonly used words, all or nothing mentality, poor sense of time, sensory processing disorders, financial problems, anxiety, uncontrollable fidgeting, hyper fixations, mood swings... do you get the picture??

An ADHDer is a perfectionist without the capability of motivating oneself to achieve that perfection. We're in this state of anxiety and self-doubt, and we feel worse every minute. We are not purposefully ignoring you. We are not dismissing you. Out of sight is out of mind. If we don't see you, you don't exist. I know that sounds harsh, but it's true.

I've had a lot of people message me on Facebook and even tell me in person how much they appreciate my posts, as silly as they are. Sometimes they tell me, *"Oh, Amanda, you're so brave for sharing your story."* No, I'm really not. It isn't noble - I'm practically uncontrollably compelled to share. But those messages do make me feel good, so keep them coming, please!

Remember those hacks I was talking about for executive dysfunction? Well, one of the things that we do a lot is lose things. So then we'll put something in a safe place, but then we can't remember the safe place. We went to Disney four years ago, and I hid my keys in case my mom needed to drive my car, and I still haven't found them. Who's with me?

And then there's the urge to use parentheses in every sentence. I want to use parentheses, ellipses, bold type, and italics in everything I write. And not being able to use emojis in this manuscript has *KILLLLLED* me! As I was editing this book, I went through and took a lot of that stuff out. Then I said, *"Nope, Amanda, not today. You're gonna write it as you talk it and write it as you think it."* So, if you have a problem with ellipses and parentheses and things like that, you have probably really struggled through this book. My English-teaching perfect grammar and punctuation-loving mama has probably gagged throughout it! Sorry, Mama...

I saw the perfect analogy recently. When someone rapidly fires questions, or even a question out of the blue requiring a definitive answer, it's like our brains go into computer update mode. The answer is in there, but we just spin and spin and spin, and often ultimately end up simply shutting down so that we can restart clean. That may make zero sense to you, but it resonated with me like crazy. An innocent and simple question like *"Who's picking Parker up from soccer?"* can send my brain into a hyper spin and often results in *"Babe, I don't know, I haven't thought that far ahead yet"* when, in fact, I have. I just can't put the puzzle pieces together on the spot. It's bizarre. Ask me about strategically marketing a home, and I can formulate a thorough, cohesive plan in two minutes. I can lay out the next 30 days and exactly what needs to happen. But ask me about a day-to-day personal task, and I freeze.

It's so frustrating, and man, am I glad to hear there are others out there with the same hurdles. If I had a dollar for every time I've said to

Bradley, *"Give me a few to work it out - I can't think that far ahead right now,"* I could buy a lifetime supply of gas. This is another reason he's a saint. He's a planner and married not just to a non-planner by nature but someone who goes into update and restart mode when asked to plan ahead. It has to be brutal for him. Your desktop goes into update mode and says it needs a few minutes to restart. Then a few minutes turn into 45. Once it updates, though, it hums. That's exactly it.

***

When I first started posting on Facebook, I was big on lists. So, to wrap up, I'm gonna put some of my lists in here just to tie a little bow on things. I have already touched on a lot of this stuff, but I feel like I need to pay homage to my Facebook posts since they are where this book originated.

One of the first lists I did was Common Traits of ADHD'ers, and I had in parentheses, "I've done every single one of these daily for years, and I just thought I was a hot mess."

One - sensory sensitivities. "Bradley Shore, if you touch me one more time, I'm going to jack-slap you. I love you, though."

Two - a bubbly, quirky personality. Yes, definitely quirky. I mean, I got the Kramer Award at work.

Three - clear standards. It's black or white, and gray doesn't exist.

Four - reliving conversations and regretting how things were handled. Often beating yourself up for being too nice instead of the other way around daily, and man, can I think of zingy comebacks later!

Five - forgetfulness. "Mama, I'll text you a reminder." My poor kids.

Six - hyper fixation. Man, can I get in the zone at work.

Seven - thinking in absolutes. I can't finish that today, so why even begin?

Eight - good and frequent world-changing ideas, but where do I start?

Nine - fatigue, burnout, depressive shutdown. Praise God for a husband and kids who give me quiet time regularly.

Ten - impulsivity. Hello, driving to Georgia and back in a day to pick up a gift.

Eleven - tripping all the time, and it's usually over the air. My poor knees and shins.

Twelve - not performing daily, mundane tasks because they're overwhelming. There are days I literally can't boil water, much less get a meal cooked.

Thirteen - getting up 14 times to create the perfect work environment. I go to work early because I like to get settled before the day begins.

Coffee made, extra water bottle handy, bathroom visit, locate readers and blue lights, create checklists, run computer clean up software (daily...), etc.

Fourteen - perfectionism. I'll draft and redraft an email eleven times before I send it.

Fifteen - obsessive note taker. It's the only way I can keep houses, conversations, etc., straight and, "Oh! That's good! I need to remember that one!"

Sixteen - poor time management. In my case, it's over-compensation by being early everywhere, and if I'm right on time, I get nauseous.

Seventeen - misplacing things. I found four other things I'd been missing when looking for my glasses. Hashtag Brightside!

Eighteen - this is too much information, but holding my bladder too long and barely making it every day. I warned you it was too much information.

Nineteen - not shutting cabinets, turning off lights, etc. I go to the kitchen to get a cup. So, I get the cup, and then in my mind, I'm done with the task, and closing the cabinet door doesn't even occur to me.

Twenty - poor sleep, so frequent napping, so then more poor sleep, and just give me ten quiet minutes, please y'all.

Twenty-one - putting off simple tasks forever. I've had "order contacts" on a sticky note for over two months, and guess what? I'm out of contacts.

Twenty-two - interrupting people. I'm so excited to relate to you that I cannot *NOT* interrupt and finish your sentence for you.

Twenty-three - the obsession of the moment. My most obvious one recently has been Bogg bags. So. Many. Bags.

Twenty-four - scarcity mindset. They may discontinue that lipstick, so I need to order twelve.

Twenty-five - joint popping. How do you not do that? Don't you feel the pressure?

Twenty-six - stimming, like hair twirling, skin picking, etc. This then makes you look like an airhead, which is as far from the truth as anything because that brain is full, and there is zero space for air.

Twenty-seven - favorite expressions and habits like speaking in hashtags and referring to oneself in the third person ("hashtag bright side," and "Amanda doesn't camp").

***

Another list I did was things you might hear an ADHD'er say (specifically, this one).

Number one - where is my phone, book, keys, etc.? I know I put it right here.

Number two - I'm so hot. Is anyone else hot?

Number three - Do you hear that? What's that sound? Wait, you don't hear that?

Number four - Wait, what was I doing?

Number five - I'm sorry, what? Say that again? I didn't hear you.

Number six - Well, we were at the home inspection, and wait, what was I talking about?

Number seven - Really? I have zero memory of that.

Number eight - So there was this house. Wait, did I already tell you this story?

Number nine - Oh, look at my sparkly ring!

Number ten - Yes, yes, yes! I sooo get that. Oh, wait, sorry to interrupt. You weren't finished yet. Wait, yes, I so get that. Oh, sorry. I'll let you finish. Yes, did I tell you about it? Oh, man. So sorry. Please keep going.

Number eleven - I know, like, I totally agree with that. Yes, for sure. Oh, wait, for real. Yes, wait. Am I talking too much?

Number twelve - Why did I come in here?

Number thirteen - No, no, no. There's always a bright side.

Number fourteen - Man, I need a nap. My brain is exhausted.

Number fifteen - Gosh, that is so bright, loud, etc.

Number sixteen - Why can't I get this? Why is this so easy for everyone else?

Number 17 - Something isn't sitting right here. I'm not buying it.

***

And then my final list... things heard in an ADHD household. Bless my poor husband and kids.

Number one — Mama, Worth is on the porch. I can hear him just by seeing him (Elliott, as we are pulling up the driveway).

Number two - Why are you putting the chips in the fridge? (Bradley, as I'm putting the French onion dip in the cabinet).

Number three - I'm out of contacts. Yes, I've known for a month. I was running out, but I never did call. Calling takes effort.

Number four - Can you call me? I can't find my phone.

Number five - Did you pay the bill? Yes, I paid the bill. Are you sure? I swear I paid the bill. Ugh... I didn't MAIL the bill.

Number six - Mama's taking a nap.

Number seven - You have to pretend she isn't here, Worth; she's working (my poor kids).

Number eight - If you touch me again, Bradley Shore, so help me, I will jack-slap you across the room.

Number nine - This is my couch. That's your couch.

Number ten - Everybody look for Mama's keys!

Number eleven - Babe, you sent me to the wrong place (Bradley when I gave him the wrong address).

Number twelve - Don't stress, I have AAA on speed dial!

Number thirteen - I didn't sleep well. My mind wouldn't stop spinning.

Number fourteen - Why do you get up so early?

Number fifteen - Which pile, Mama? That pile! Mama, there are eleven piles here.

Number sixteen - How do you know I'm the one who opened it? Well, Babe, the lid is crooked.

Number seventeen - Did you all hear that? What is that? Seriously, you didn't hear that?

Number eighteen - Mama, stop interrupting. Please let me talk.

Number nineteen - No, Mama, that isn't what I was gonna say. Let me finish.

Number twenty - I've been talking all day. I don't want to talk anymore.

Number twenty-one - Let me just stop you right there. If this is going to make me sad or tick me off, I don't want to hear it. I'll dwell on it all day.

Number twenty-two - Bubba, stop clicking the pen. It's driving me nuts.

Number twenty-three - I just heard you tell your client not to worry. So why are you worrying so much, Mama?

Number twenty-four - Is practice at twelve or two?

Number twenty-five - Oh, man. Supper. I had four appointments today. Can we just eat cereal? I'm drained.

And finally, my favorite - "I know. She's a rock star. I just wish she could see that" (Bradley on the phone talking to a friend).

Thank Yous

I can't let the opportunity pass to thank some folks, and if I miss you, I am so sorry. I have been putting off doing this for that very reason—I am terrified I will miss someone!

To Lindsay, all I can say is, BLESS. You worked with me for years, way before ADHD in women was discussed, and oh, how your mind must have been blown when I would squirrel 2600 times a day. And you worked for me before I knew the real estate models I follow now, so "mercy goodness" is all I can say. I can never thank you enough for handling me so well.

Bridgette – Okay, here is another "bless your heart." You were with me as I was learning those aforementioned models, and you did your best to help me fit my chaos into them—all while keeping it real! How in the world did you do that? I look back on my business and see you in so many integral moves. THANK YOU!

Sonja – I said I'd include you, so here you go. Nah, that isn't all. You unknowingly encouraged me at a time when I was thinking of throwing in the towel. When you walked up at that recital rehearsal, I was typing, "I just can't do this," to my publisher. Your excitement got me going again. I love you; I mean it!

Jodie – You were our team's assistant when I received the diagnosis, and to say that zero "surprise" registered on your face when I told you would be an understatement! You handled me so well before, but in those first few weeks, when my diagnosis frustrated me more than anything, your steady "we got this" attitude gave me hope. Thank you so much.

Jennifer – How in the world does a spreadsheet lover whose attention to detail is so acute work with someone who daily says *"details, shmetails"*? I am so very grateful that the Lord (and Jeremy!) brought you into my life. You are seriously a life-changer.

This one is a blanket - To everyone who has messaged, texted, Facebooked, etc., to tell me that my posts helped you in some way, thank you. This is for you. I can't tell you the number of times I would make a post, and then the devil would jump on my back and have me convinced that it was TMI or embarrassing or would bring reproach on my family, and lo and behold, as I went to delete it, I would see a message saying keep it up. I pray this book helps you understand and love yourselves and your near and dears even more!

Lisa - I can't even begin to thank you or tell you how much I love and appreciate you, so I won't even try anything other than to say thank you for being my sister.

To Bradley - You made this happen. That day in Fancy Gap when I gave you some of my rough drafts—knowing you would tell me if I was nutso—and then, after reading them, you leaned down and said, "I think you need to write this book"—is a memory I go back to over and over. And, oh, what a year we have had. Your grit and determination have inspired me beyond belief, and I know beyond a shadow of a doubt that together we can face anything. Thank you for being my true partner in all things. You have dealt with so many repercussions from this crazy condition, and I don't know anyone who could have ridden the roller coaster as well as you have. You are a mighty man of God, and I love you so much. IAYAYAM. Always.

Finally, to **Candy** - You know why.

Acknowledgements

I have been cognizant the whole time I have been putting this book together that I may very well be plagiarizing some things. I am the daughter of a high school English teacher, for goodness' sake! I was raised on bibliographies and annotations! Anyhow, if I have, it is completely unintentional. As you know, we ADHDers love to ruminate, and I do not doubt that there were certain articles, podcasts, and Facebook posts from others that I read and listened to so often that I internalized some of the verbiage and then made it "mine." There is no way I can go back in line by line and give credit where it is due, so I pray doing so on this page will suffice.

A HUGE thank you to Tracey Otsuka for your podcast, ADHD for Smart Ass Women (excuse the French!). I discovered you immediately following my diagnosis, and oh, the mornings I would drive to work either laughing hysterically or crying because *yes, someone gets it!* You made sense of so many things, from dental issues to giving things a name that I could never explain. Thank you, thank you, thank you.

Gaurdian.com had an article last year that talked about the "lost girls." That was one of the first things I read (originally shared by Lauire

Christofano!). I have no doubt that I have repeated some things from that article verbatim. It nailed us lost girls. 100%.

Chadd.org and your "How the Gender Gap Leaves Girls and Women Undertreated for ADHD"—man. So good. "Frenzied, Frazzled, and Overwhelmed" was also amazing.

There are so many other social media accounts, to name a few:

Little Miss Lionheart

Adhd_things

Adhdmemes

ADHD Interrupted

Numerous TikTok accounts, including Cullen and Katie, Dani Donovan, and Coby Watts.

About the Author

Amanda is a wife, mama, daughter, sister, and real estate professional still trying to figure out what God's will is for her life. She lives in Yadkin County, NC with her saint of a husband, their 3 perfectly perfect for them children, and anywhere from four to six dogs depending on the day. Her husband and kids have 12 chickens, and she eats the eggs but refuses to claim them as hers. She loves Jesus, writing, good books, road trips, animals, and seeing the best in people. When not writing, you can find her napping, loving on her real estate clients, or attending her kids' many activities.

Printed in Dunstable, United Kingdom

76423179R00082